Becoming Genevieve

GENEVIEVE DAVIS

Disclaimer: The author bears no responsibility for any consequences resulting from the use of information provided in this book. Please use all information at your own risk. No part of this publication may be reproduced or transmitted in any form without the express permission of the author.

Becoming Genevieve

An Extraordinary
True Story of
Believing in Magic

Genevieve Davis

CONTENTS

PART 3 THE DARKEST HOUR IS
RIGHT BEFORE THE DAWN

PART 4 FIRST DAY OF MY NEW LIFE

PART 5 AND THE UNIVERSE RESPONDED

What's the Deal?

It turns out there is a secret after all. There is a secret to having a truly exceptional life. It's nothing like the film or the book of that name. Not even remotely similar. But it's better. Far better.

You know that stuff all the really spiritual people speak about? Your authentic, higher or true self, your divine essence, universal mind, Big Mind, and all that jazz? Guess what? It's all real. It's all true. And it's the secret to creating anything you could ever wish to create.

There is a place inside of you that is infinitely powerful, infinitely loving, and that feels incredible. When you are connected to this place, every problem you have ever had disappears, life feels exquisite, and you know, as sure as you've ever known anything, that *you* are impossibly perfect. From this place, you can, with minimal effort, create pretty much anything you could ever want.

This is not wishful thinking.

It is not just a New Age, flowery, hippy thing.

It is not just motivational rhetoric.

It is not just a story. It is not opinion. It is not theory.

It is true. 100% true.

Just imagine for a moment, a world where all the bad memories, the depression, the anxiety, the black moods, the nagging worries... imagine a world where none of those things has any real power to hurt you. Imagine *you* but with no vulnerability to any of these destructive thought patterns. Imagine what you'd be capable of in a world where fear didn't stop you doing *anything* you wanted to do. Imagine a world where every single one of your problems, no matter how severe it seems, could melt or transform before your eyes, revealing itself to be no problem at all. Imagine receiving fantastical insights that allow you to solve any troublesome issue with perfect ease. Imagine a world where depression no longer has the power to ruin your day, where fears and insecurities no longer have any power to stop you doing what you love, where disease and death no longer make you afraid, where anxiety *no longer bothers you*, where mental illness *does not exist*.

Can you get a sense of that? Imagine how free you'd be.

It sounds like a pie in the sky promise, doesn't it? It sounds like I've lost my mind. I promise you, I'm speaking with pure integrity. I've never been so sure in my life.

I Have Manifested My Wildest Dreams...

All my life, I've searched for first-hand knowledge of the 'greater truths' about the human experience. Fuelled by a voracious appetite for self-help, I have read more spiritual books than is probably healthy. Over the years, I've heard gurus and ordinary folk talk of fantastic enlightenment experiences, in which they were able to comprehend the reality of the true self and the illusory nature of the material world. I heard some say the answers we seek can be found within us. I heard others say we are already perfect, whole and complete. I read we don't *feel* love, we don't *give* love, we *are* love. And, once we get a glimpse of the reality beyond the illusion, we'll see these things as truth.

Different forms. A lot of different people. Same message.

The most inspiring books I read over the years seemed always to have been written by people who had undergone a sudden, spontaneous and profound awakening after which they never saw the world in quite the same way again. White light, rushes and blasts of joy, being struck dumb, voices from God, explosions of inexplicable bliss. I read about a monk who sold his Ferrari and a young

9

German called Eckhart Tolle who was so blown away by his awakening that he sat on a park bench for two years, doing nothing but basking in the ecstasy of his perfect existence.

So where was *my* enlightenment moment? Where was my awakening? After all, I had read the books. I had meditated. I had gone on retreats and learned techniques. I read even more, and meditated a lot more, and waited and waited and waited for the thunderbolt moment.

But it never came.

Obviously, I was doing it wrong. No matter how much I meditated and studied and followed the techniques, I couldn't do what those other spiritual people could do. I couldn't see what they saw. Perhaps I never would. Perhaps I never *could*.

But while I may not have had a spiritual awakening, I did get something almost as fantastic. You see, over the years, I developed the ability to make things happen. I could effect change. I could attract material possessions. I was able to create a better experience of the world. I had mastered what some people call 'manifesting'.

For those who aren't familiar with my earlier works, I'll introduce myself. My name (a pseudonym) is Genevieve Davis. As Genevieve, I've written four books on the subject of making things happens, getting what you want, and improving your life by making changes to you, your attitude, beliefs and demeanour. Some people call this 'manifesting', but because I never really knew how it worked, I've always preferred to call this process *magic*.

What I really wanted to know was how my own knowledge of what I called 'magic' tied in with these elusive 'greater truths' about the human experience. But there was a problem: many of the writers I respected dismissed the whole idea of manifesting out of hand. And while I knew there had to be truth in these other, more esoteric writings, I also had the truth of my own experience, of 'making things happen'. My own experience surely counted far more than the words of anyone else, no matter how much I respected them, no matter how spiritual they were.

I wanted to be happy. I wanted to awaken. I wanted enlightenment. I wanted to know the truth. But I couldn't dismiss the *way things looked to me*. And the way it looked to me was that by thinking, acting, behaving, and believing in a certain way, I had made tons of money, attracted a partner, made friends — in short, that I had used what I liked to call *magic* to manifest what outwardly appeared to be an exceptional life. Those things had actually happened. They had happened to *me*.

But what was the relationship between these two 'truths'? Between magic, and the bigger spiritual picture. Were they incompatible? Did they invalidate each other? Was one superior or prior to the other? Instinctively, intuitively I felt they were connected.

Now I know the truth.

During this time, I have discovered that my experience with and writing about magic were just the preliminaries. They were just the beginning. Magic and manifesting were the first essential steps, paving the way for an incredible journey that has led to an understanding of life, the universe and reality that is so perfect, so delightful it is mind-blowing.

It is all good. In fact, it's bloody *perfect*.

The cool thing is, I can see why those previous techniques for experiencing enlightenment had been ineffective for me. And it's partly *because* the authors had written in such eloquent and thrilling ways about the fantasticalness of their miraculous transformations. When it was time for my own transformation, it came *gradually*. And it was when I stopped looking for, and longing for, and demanding that thunderbolt moment, that things started to change.

All those years I assumed I had been getting it wrong.

And I had been getting it right all along.

And, as it turns out, my hunch was right: awakening and manifestation *are* connected. How unfathomably fantastic is that? My search this past year has been the investigation of this connection. Having made the discovery of a lifetime, my only goal now is to tell you all about it. My intention was to write a book that bridged the gap between Eckhart Tolle's *The Power of Now* and Michael Singer's beautiful *The Untethered Soul* with my own understanding of the way that magic and manifestation seem to work. You can be the judge of whether I've succeeded.

I must warn you. This book is largely memoir. I tried very hard to limit the 'I, I, I' business but I'm afraid it will be 'all about me' for quite some time. If first-person memoirs aren't your thing, please put the book down and turn to another. But if you can grant me an audience, I think you'll understand why I write about myself so much. It's not because I think my life has been particularly interesting or noteworthy. It's not because I'm very famous. It's because I want to prove to you that everything I say is the truth. This is a faithful account of some of the key points of my life over the past ten years or so. If you could be bothered, you could verify pretty much everything I'm about to say. For the most part, I haven't even changed the names and places.

In this book I'm going to tell the story of my personal journey to this inner wonderland. It is less a step-by-step instruction manual and more of a signpost, gently pointing to this source of infinite power and wellbeing within you.

Keep reading. Let me tell you my story.

It will show you, more than ever, why I *believe in magic.*

PART 1
BEFORE GENEVIEVE

1. It's 2010 and Life Sucks

What a sad, crappy pile of crap life turned out to be. It was 2010, and I was depressed. Too bored even to feel sorry for myself. Another miserable dropout. Another middle-aged woman living a life of unfulfilled potential. A statistic. How dull. How positively mundane.

Self-loathing? No, far from it. Self-loathing would almost glamorise what I felt about myself. My life was far too dull to warrant something as extravagant as self-loathing. What I felt was more like utter self-indifference.

I wasn't loathsome; I was irrelevant. Absolutely and completely insignificant.

Would I be forgotten after I died? The question was moot: I'd already been forgotten.

Once upon a time I could get by, impressing people with my intelligence. As a doctoral student in philosophy, I worked as a part-time undergraduate seminar leader. But as the years went by, the part-time work never made way for a full-time position, and being a professional smartarse no longer paid the bills. I was just another of the over-qualified, under-experienced, menially employed.

The cute, flirty, 20-something girl, talking about Wittgenstein at parties had turned into a 40-year-old, overweight has-been. Or more like a never-was. An intellectual waster. A bore.

You're probably thinking I spend a lot of time talking about myself. And putting myself down. Talking about myself and putting myself down: the two most un-endearing characteristics of the chronically depressed. Self-obsession and self-criticism. Oh, and a tendency toward overly dramatic and complex descriptions of one's miserable state. You see, by using big words I can draw even greater attention to the unfairness of the situation, just to prove to you that *I wasn't supposed to turn out this way, you know?*

Don't worry. This pity party isn't going to go on forever. But I must warn you: it does go on for a little while longer yet.

It was 5.15 am, and I had slept in. *Slept in! At 5.15 am!* Still sick with sleep, I walked right past the kitchen to the bathroom. Even if I had had time for breakfast, I couldn't possibly have eaten at that time of the morning. A quick tooth-brushing and a bit of mascara were all I had time for. Work started at six, and I needed to be early.

I got into my Ford Ka, and no matter how hard I tried to look past it, I couldn't help but notice the tax disc. It was in date with still four months to run. I wasn't stupid enough not to show a valid tax disc. But the sight of the disc reminded me that I was stupid enough not to have a valid MOT. You see, an MOT is a trust-based tax. The government trusted me to get a valid MOT. I trusted them not to find out I didn't have one.

Unlike a tax disc, back in 2010, there was no external evidence for an MOT. No disc to show. No way to tell this car didn't have the legally-required certificate of roadworthiness other than asking to see the certificate. No way, of course, other than the bald tyres, the smashed-in licence plate, and the crack in the windscreen. Of course, I wanted to drive a legal car. I needed to drive a safe car. But I couldn't afford the MOT. And I couldn't get to work without a car. And if I didn't go to work, I couldn't earn the money to pay for the MOT. Is that a catch-22 or a vicious circle? Perhaps it's just a shit situation. I'm not sure.

God, I must sound so dull. *I* think I sound dull, so you must be bored stupid by now. And there goes the self-deprecation again. Sorry, that must be so irritating. I'll try and stop it.

I am a loved, loving and lovable human being. I am whole and complete.

Yeah, right.

I got to work 20 minutes early and touched my card on the card reader to enter the factory. A large, indeterminately foreign security guard nodded as I went through the turnstile.

The company cafeteria was already full of workers, eating breakfasts of bacon sandwiches and cake. Most were migrant workers from Hungary, Poland or Lithuania. There were quite a few from Pakistan and only a handful of British workers, mostly middle-aged women. Everyone turned up early for the same reason. Breakfast may seem impossible at 5 am but tempting 45 minutes later. To be honest, I was now starving. After ordering a coffee, I sat down and pulled out a shop-bought packet of croissants to eat with my coffee. I would have warmed them in the factory-provided microwave had there not been a queue. I ate the croissants cold. God, the coffee was bad. I took a big gulp, scanning around my senses for any evidence of a caffeine hit and finding none. What was the excuse for such bad coffee, I often wondered, especially in a room full of Europeans? Surely, it was in the company's interests to keep the workers pepped up and motivated with artificial stimulation? But the workers at this factory had another way of keeping their energy levels up during their 12-hour shifts: the cafeteria did a roaring trade in cans of Red Bull.

It can take a while for a British person to get used to the idiosyncrasies of Eastern Europeans. One of the most bewildering things is the lack of smiling or laughing. It took me some time to understand that this was not an indication of surliness, unhappiness, or even seriousness. What I did come to see was how much of British joviality was nothing more than a social nicety. You may not realise it, but most of our everyday smiling and laughing is nothing more than politeness. Eastern European societies didn't have that social custom. That's the only difference.

Because let's face it, I might have smiled more than my fellow workers. I might have joked more. But happy?

Contented? I was anything but. Underneath the polite smiles and jokes, I wasn't any less grumpy than my Eastern European chums.

The warning bell rang loudly. In five minutes, the shift would officially begin. Anyone not at their workstations at the second bell would have their pay docked. As if our pay wasn't bad enough already.

If you've read *Becoming Magic,* you probably don't recognise the author of that book and this introduction as the same person. In *Becoming Magic,* I start the book with an uplifting, motivating description of the power within all of us. In this book, I start with a depressing load of self-indulgent drivel. Why? It's to draw into sharp contrast just how different my life once was. I begin this book at one of the worst points of my life.

I'd been working at the factory nearly a year. It had initially been a stopgap — a quick and easy way to bring in a bit of cash. It might have been minimum wage, but the hours were long and you could do pretty much as many days as you liked. Those hours could tot up to quite a decent wage packet, as long as you were willing to half kill yourself with exhaustion, muck up your social life, and have no fingernails left.

So temporary, emergency stopgap had turned into full-time job. I had become good at the work. I was popular with the other workers and had been noticed by the management, getting a promotion of sorts (extra responsibility for the same pay).

Once upon a time, I had had dreams of being a full-time university lecturer. Now I worked 50 hours a week packing boxes for minimum wage. My magnificent years had been and gone, and it was too late to shine. It was the greatest cliché of all.

I had wasted my life.

Twelve hours later, the delightful sound of the bell ringing signalled the end of our shift (and the beginning of the night shift). As we gleefully left our workstations, we were instantly replaced by gloomy-faced substitutes, about to start their own 12-hour shift at 6 pm.

The illegal little rust bucket of a Ford Ka, sitting alone in a corner of the carpark, now appeared to me a beacon of comfort and salvation. An oasis of familiarity. I unlocked the door and sat down gratefully in the comfy Ford driver's seat, my exhausted muscles finally being allowed to rest. I started the car, turned on the radio, and sat for a few minutes, blowing on my hands and waiting for the car to warm up a little. I drove home, put a ready meal in the microwave, and fell asleep in front of the television.

2. A Magical Childhood

Let's back up a decade or four.

As a small child, I must have appeared a little odd. Born on 31st October, I was often called 'weird' and sometimes 'witch' by the children, and even by the adults around me. For some reason, I seemed to unnerve people, bewilder them. People didn't like the way I looked at them — 'into their souls'. My auntie used to call me a 'Midwich Cuckoo' because of my piercing eyes. Generally, I was probably a little too wise-seeming, too self-contained, maybe even a little spooky. And, like many children, I could do magic.

It always seemed obvious to me that things would turn out my way if I did certain things, performed certain rituals, or said certain things. I wrote stories and spells and magic words. I'd dig in the garden for lucky stones, pick enchanted sticks from the woods to use as magic wands, wait hours to see shooting stars, and I'd speak to trees. I'd go for long walks alone along the coast to Compass Cove or down to Old Mill Creek.

That's usually when *the Glimpses* would come to me.

I can't remember when I first noticed it, but throughout my life I have had these tiny, instantaneous, profound little experiences. They are almost impossible to describe, but I'll do my best. (Apologies for the string of apparent oxymorons that you are about to read.)

These little incidents would appear like a flicker across my consciousness. A flash of knowing, of bright recognition, smiling anticipation, and bubbling excitement. They were otherworldly, yet *so* familiar. It was like I was seeing another life once lived, to be lived, or perhaps being lived right at that moment, in another place, another dimension. It was like autumn leaves underfoot, the breathless silence of midnight snow, the spicy, icy, tinkling tingle of Christmas, the smoky evening hum of a summer festival. It was something ancient, but also *now*. What *is* that?

I came to call it *The Glimpse.*

The Glimpses would come without warning and be gone almost without duration, lasting less than a fraction of a second, too fast to be even considered a moment in time. An instant. But in that instant, I could sense that all I had ever searched for — the joy, the love, the belonging, the safety — was all contained in that momentary experience. Like the closest relationship you could ever have, the safest place, like you'd just heard the best news in the world. It was bliss, grace, and excitement all rolled into one.

This same feeling sometimes arose like a joyful buzz when in company I really enjoyed. I felt it when laughing with friends, when picnicking in the park, and when deep down and dirty in nature. The Glimpses were earthy and alive. They also came reliably at Christmas, and even on Friday afternoons as I dawdled wearily back from school and realised the weekend was upon me. Best of all, I felt The Glimpse at ancient monuments, historical sites, even stately homes. The Glimpse was history. It was memory. It was Now. Like past, present, and future all in one. It felt like belonging but went way beyond. It was oneness.

The Glimpses would come, and they would go. And it seemed nothing I did could make them last longer or come more frequently. When I was happier, they came more often. When I was miserable, they didn't come at all. That's all I knew. I fantasised about a life living *inside* those moments. If I could have the experience more often, the individual moments would meet and join up, and those moments would make up my entire life — a life beyond perfection.

For most of my life, I had been searching for the source of and reason for this most delicious and elusive kind of experience.

I wonder if any of you have ever felt something similar?

My mother was widowed at the age of 27 when my father was killed in a car accident. Left alone with four children under the age of ten, she brought us all to be closer to her own family in the picturesque town of Dartmouth in Devon. Our life was one of beautiful, messy, magical chaos in a large but unkempt, unheated house full of pets and spiders. Our house was big, but it was also crumbling. In the winters we dressed in bed because our bedrooms were freezing. When we ran out of toilet paper, we often used newspaper. On Sundays, we sometimes ate the strangest food because my mother had no money until the family allowance came through on Tuesday.

But we also had a menagerie of animals, and thanks to my mother's careful management, we never went hungry. By today's standards (and by my mother's reckoning) you might say we lived in poverty. But it never felt that way at the time, and we were infused with the understanding that, while money was tight, we were capable of very great things.

From a very young age, my mother encouraged us to be extremely independent. We were cooking, washing our own clothes while still in primary school, but also earning money in our spare time, sorting out school paperwork and personal administration, making decisions at an age when most children can barely read and write.

My mother instilled in me a sense of taking absolute and complete responsibility for my own life. This meant that when something wasn't right, or when I wanted something to happen or to change, it never occurred to me to look to anyone or anything else to sort it out. When I wanted something, I tended to jump into immediate action. I was tall as an 11-year-old, and by telling people I was 14, I was able to get part-time work as a waitress, a babysitter, delivering leaflets and even working a huge hot iron press, printing t-shirts in a tourist gift shop. At age 12, I 'd saved enough money to buy a snooker table. At 14, I bought my own horse, Danny. At age 17, I paid for my own driving lessons and passed my driving test. As a teenager in the vibrant 1980s, I felt immortal, powerful and was so looking forward to the incredible life I knew I was due. And, for the first 20 or so years of my life, I felt I was able magically to create whatever I wanted.

At the age of 19, I accidentally-on-purpose became pregnant. By 20, I was a mother. By 21, I was a single mother. We haven't heard from my son's father in nearly 30 years.

I loved my little son more than it's possible to put into words. From the second he popped out with what looked like a smile on his face, Robin was the sunniest baby boy. A born artist, and reading at the age of two, Robin was just the most fantastic little human being I have ever met. He never cried and was sleeping through the night at six weeks old.

Sorry if this boasting makes you sick or envious. I am rather prone to bragging where Robin is concerned. I sometimes wonder how I ever made such a person. I never had postnatal depression, but I *did* have postnatal euphoria. Where Robin is concerned, I think I probably still have it.

When Robin was four years old, I decided it was time I went to university. With a sense of 'no one's going to stop me doing what I want to do', and still believing that I could and would do anything and everything with my life, I took my little son off to begin a new life in the University of Hertfordshire. It was just little Robbie and me against the world, changing the world, saving the world. We weren't only mother and son. We were friends.

I was unstoppable. I was intelligent. I was slim. I was reasonably attractive. And I was never, ever going to use my single motherhood as an excuse to stop me doing anything. My fantastic life was about to begin. What could possibly go wrong?

3. University, Insomnia, and Unsuitable Men

What was it that led this dreamy, magical child, confident teenager, happy young mother into a minimum wage job at the wrong side of 40, lost and miserable?

Shortly before going to university in 1993, I began a particularly toxic and eventually abusive relationship that went on for some years. My boyfriend (let's call him Rick) had a terrible temper and was very unpredictable, often going from smiling and laughing to dark fury in a heartbeat.

I really cannot explain to you why I chose to stay with a man I didn't particularly like and never loved. But perhaps it was because I didn't want to be alone. Robin and I had a lot of fun together. But once he was in bed, I would feel quite isolated and I came to depend on Rick's company. Spending time with a bully was better than spending an entire weekend alone. At least that's how it felt at the time. Without my even noticing it was happening, the relationship became abusive, and I got more and more worn down. It didn't even register with me when things turned violent.

But that's not all. Something was to happen that would dominate and devastate my life for the next 15 years. In my first year at university, I started having sleepless nights. One bad night turned to two, then three. Weeks of poor sleep turned to months as the relentless affliction of insomnia took hold of my life. I fell upon the mercy of doctors, therapists, and sleeping pills. But this only seemed to make the matter worse. I would lie awake at night, crying, praying, raging, begging someone — anyone — to help me. But no one ever came. All of my previous empowerment and independence and taking responsibility were gone, and I began to lose control of my life.

For years, I threw myself under the umbrella of academia. I discovered that in the relative safety of university, I could shine, if only in that sheltered, somewhat unreal environment. After finishing top of the year with a first-class degree in philosophy, I was offered some part-time teaching work to undergrads. After getting my masters degree, I started one, then two, then *three* PhDs.

Are you impressed by my academic prowess? Don't be.

You see, I was a self-confirmed chronic insomniac and would do anything to get a good night's sleep. The academic lifestyle meant that I didn't have to get out of bed and go to work in the morning. Getting a full-time job would be far too risky, given my terrible sleep patterns. All this academic study was really just an effective way to hide away from life, because one of the best (and worst) things about being an academic is that it gives you a permanent excuse. When asked *What do you do?* you can always reply, 'I'm doing a PhD', and wait for the impressed reactions. Now, 'doing a PhD' might involve writing a fascinating and ground-breaking piece of hugely important research. It might be the most exciting and stimulating time of your life, a time when you push your intellect to its limit, travel the world presenting papers, meeting the most interesting and brilliant people.

Or, it might consist of reading the odd article over a coffee in Starbucks, underlining the sentences you like best, and scribbling notes in the margins of secondhand books. It might mean getting drunk at conferences and hanging around at the British Library, reading newspapers. It might mean being semi-permanently de-registered, just reregistering now and again so you don't lose your student status. Yeah, that pretty much sums up my PhD years. But 'doing a PhD' did give me a certain acceptable status in society. It meant

a) I was quite clever (and so provided me with instant justification for my existence); and

b) I had no obligation to go out and get a real job.

So, for someone effectively hiding from reality, 'doing a PhD' was the perfect ~~excuse~~ career choice.

I was still going out with Rick, and the relationship was going from bad to worse, becoming stormier and more unpredictable. I was also becoming worried about the effect of this unhealthy environment on my young son. Still unable to sleep, and desperately unhappy, I fell into a deep depression. It seemed to me the world was not behaving in anything like a supportive way. Life was just happening *to* me. Car breakdowns, a Peeping Tom, a stalker, and two burglaries visited me while I languished at the University of Hertfordshire. I spent much of that time feeling utterly powerless. I had become a victim. Money was always desperately tight, and I had to take work as a cleaner and do a summer on the tills in McDonalds to raise some cash. I was a victim: of insomnia, of an abusive boyfriend, of circumstances, of poverty. At one point I became so stressed I began losing my hair.

I distinctly remember one evening toward the end of my time at Hertfordshire. My best friend at the time, Victoria, came over to my student accommodation. She had brought a candle-making kit with her. We spent the evening making hideous brown candles, closely resembling dog poo. That evening we laughed so much our tummies hurt. And I remember the sudden, startling realisation I had that night: it was the first time I could remember laughing, *at all*, in years.

In 1997, Rick and I moved away from Hertfordshire to Brighton to start the second of my PhDs, at the University of Sussex. It was there I met Nadja, a person of exceptional and unconventional intelligence, the woman who would go on to become my best female friend. She remains so to this day. But even Nadja couldn't make up for the misery I was experiencing at home, with Rick and the still-sleepless nights.

It only took two months of living with Rick on a daily basis to make the decision to leave him, once and for all. With no money and nowhere to live, I borrowed money from my sister Lisa, and Robin and I moved into a shoddy maisonette.

Hang on a second!

This wasn't how things were supposed to turn out. Where had the old me gone? Where was the bright young thing who was going to rule the world, cure cancer and marry a prince? I was once able to get whatever I wanted. Now, I couldn't make *anything* happen. I couldn't even make myself sleep. My wonderful life was turning out to be a bit of a disappointment.

But at least I was still young. I had decades left to start my *real* life.

4. My First Magical Friends

While living in Brighton, I met and fell in love with Ian, the man who would go on to become my husband. We married two years later, in the beautiful St Petrox church on the edge of a cliff, looking out to sea on the outskirts of Dartmouth. It was the best wedding I had ever been to, with dancing and laughing all night. But insomnia still tormented me, along with bouts of depression and black moods. On the night before my wedding I didn't sleep for even one minute.

It was while married that I began to dabble in self-help, reading books and trying out techniques, all with the intention of improving my sleep. I remember the first books I ever bought — Richard Carlson's *Stop Thinking, Start Living* and *You Can Heal Your Life* by the wonderful Louise Hay.

Besides the immediate issue of sorting out my sleep, there was a deeper, more fundamental reason for my interest in spirituality and self-help. During the bad times of my 20s, it was the *Glimpses* that kept me going, that feeling I would get standing at an ancient site, in an old church, or at Christmas, that *magic*. Those delightful flashes of perfection seemed to me to hold the promise of another life, another world, where everything was brighter, where depression and insomnia didn't exist, and where I was welcomed with open arms.

If anyone had asked me at the time — if a fairy godmother had waved her wand, if a genie had popped out of a bottle — my dearest wish would be to *live life in The Glimpse.*

My search for this elusive experience took me to some pretty weird places.

I longed to find a group of people with the best and strongest connection with the earth, with nature, with history. People who could help me understand The Glimpse. People who wouldn't give me a blank look when I mentioned it and might even have experienced something similar. It seemed to me that pagans, with their candles and their rituals, their open minds, their respect for nature, and their sitting around next to the bonfire in the moonlight would surely have what I was looking for.

Finding a local pagan group was easily done in a place such as Brighton, home of the alternative and bohemian, the weird and wonderful. It took only a few emails, and I had an invitation to the Brighton Pagans group. I remember my first meeting, in a pub aptly named the Sun, Moon and Stars. I walked into the room to find a dozen or more of the oddest-looking people I had ever seen. Shaved heads, blond dreadlocks, facial piercings and tattoos were everywhere. There were also floaty dresses, jingling bangles, and t-shirts with transfers of wolves howling at the moon. A faint whiff of patchouli was in the air. I was introduced to the group:

Star, Red, Dragon, Orc, Tun, Flop, Chance, Prof, Tabby, Starling, Cinders, Cosmic, Moggie.

Amongst these colourful characters, there was one particular couple that caught my attention. A small, captivating woman with long, bright-red hair, and a tall, thin boy. In a room full of the weirdest oddbods you could ever wish to meet, these two stood out as possessing a sort of intelligent confidence. It turned out Jo was a Wiccan. She considered herself a witch, had been a member of a coven, and did spells to bring about change. But *please* don't imagine this meant she was some devil worshipper. She wasn't. Not even close. She was and still is, a very, very good person. She cares about things, about people, animals and the world. She campaigns for change and makes good things happen. She is clever and funny, and she became a good friend.

Jo introduced me to the tall, thin boy, who can't have been more than 19 or 20, her best friend, my namesake, the incredible Matthew Davis.

Matthew George Patrick Davis. Fifteen years my junior. Intriguing. Different. Matthew was quietly and understatedly eccentric. But like all good eccentrics, he had no idea of the unusualness of himself. Matt was so profoundly unpretentious it almost seemed affected. He was one of the most fascinating people I had ever met, and it was after being inspired by this exceptional human being that I decided on Genevieve Davis as the pen name for my magical books.

But that's a story for another time.

It was Jo who first alerted me to the idea that manifesting (in the self-help sense of the word) was akin to magic. What she actually used to say was, 'A magic spell is just an intention'. It was an idea I'd always liked but had never really taken seriously. Only many years later would those words turn out to hold great significance for me.

Through Jo and Matt, I spent a memorable ten days working at Glastonbury Festival. It was there I began a lifelong love affair with Celtic music, thanks to the Peatbog Faeries, my favourite ever live band. The joy I felt listening to that band was so intense, so ecstatic, when the show was over I jumped the barrier to congratulate the musicians and was forcibly removed by bouncers. Listening to the Peatbog Faeries was a peak experience, but it didn't really help me in my quest to live in The Glimpse. I could hardly spend my whole life at a music concert. Plus, I discovered another thing at Glastonbury: I really, *really* hated camping!

When I returned from Glastonbury, my husband, Ian, eyed me suspiciously. 'Was it awful? How was it, sharing toilets with ten thousand people? You need a shower, by the way,' he said.

You may already know that the journey of self-discovery is much harder if your life partner isn't along for the ride. Ian certainly wasn't interested in coming with me on this trip, and for a long time he was positively hostile to my new 'spiritual' interests. It must have seemed my life was going off in a direction that he couldn't understand. By the time

Ian began to accept that my interest in spiritual matters wasn't merely a passing phase, it was too late.

He had always worked away a lot, sometimes arriving home in the small hours of Sunday morning, leaving again for work on Monday. Because of this, we never developed a proper partnership. I had my life, and he had his, and those two lives trundled by independently of each other. He began to seem more like a stranger to me every time he came home.

When the first flush of love faded, it turned out there was nothing left. No partnership or reliance or trust had had a chance to develop. The honeymoon period was over, and there was nothing to replace it. I tried desperately to rekindle the love I had once felt for him, even seeking out a hypnotherapist to hypnotise me into loving him again. But every therapist told me this was impossible. You cannot brainwash someone into loving someone else. You cannot fake love.

I remember the exact moment I knew the marriage was over. We were going into town, and Ian tried to take my hand so that we could walk hand in hand. I recoiled from his touch. Right then, I knew I couldn't hold his hand ever again. He had become alien to me.

5. Adventures in London

The split was acrimonious. But although he was furious at me for leaving him, Ian didn't fight and bought me out of the property in which we lived. I received £110,000 in settlement for the divorce. It was the greatest sum of money I had ever had. And, unbelievably, that's when things started to go from bad to worse.

With my newfound freedom, and with enough money to start again in a different town, I set out in earnest to find The Glimpse. The first step on this quest was giving up my philosophy PhD (the second PhD I had attempted). With my typical black and white thinking, and my tendency to grand, overdramatic gestures, I burned my doctoral thesis. And I don't mean that metaphorically; I literally set fire to it. Every note, every paper, every article went on a ceremonial bonfire in my back garden. I remember it didn't feel quite as good as I'd expected.

The burning of my thesis was symbolic, not a mere temper tantrum. It represented a rejection of a particular way of thinking, almost a rejection of rationality. My branch of philosophy was very analytic, involving the creation of step-by-step, watertight arguments. Philosophy had started out as an entertaining way to stretch my mind, like doing crossword puzzles. It had also driven me slightly bonkers. In its questioning and unravelling of ideas, its reduction of everything to first principles, and its incessant, crippling, stagnating logic, it had twisted my mind into a knot, leaving it stuck and exhausted. When my supervisor told me to go through my thesis and remove every adjective, I realised my philosophy days were over.

But I wasn't ready to leave the protection of academia. Not ready to get a 'real' job, I started a completely new, *third* PhD, at the University of East London. The subject was prehistoric anthropology, and I would be studying the societies that built the ancient monuments of Wessex, Stonehenge and Avebury stone circles. I had always loved visiting those places, in part because those sorts of ancient sites prompted the strongest and most regular Glimpses.

It was going to be amazing. I would make the best friends at this new university, be welcome and wanted, and have the time of my life. I was going to commune with monuments, their makers, with history, and time itself. It was perfect. I would find all I had been looking for, I was sure of it. I packed up my bags, and with my Siamese cat, Chipper, in tow, I left Brighton for London. Robin, now 18 and attending Northbrook College, had chosen to stay behind with my mother.

When I arrived in London, I truly believed my real life was about to start. I think I had some notion that I'd step off the train, shouting and waving, 'I'm here!' and hundreds of cool new friends would rush up and take me excitedly by the hand. 'We've been waiting for you!' they'd say. 'Come with us!' and they'd whisk me off to the first of a thousand parties.

It didn't turn out quite like that.

I know many people absolutely love London and wouldn't consider living anywhere else. But I found the city angry and unfriendly. Everyone was rushing to get somewhere, no one looking anybody else in the eye, everyone speaking a different language and never to each other. For a woman more used to the simple open friendliness of Devon and the easy acceptance of Brighton — where everyone thanked bus drivers, allowed dogs in cafés, and where no one could quite believe their luck in living in such a place — London was a bit of a shock. And, to my utter dismay, I didn't feel *welcome* in London.

Worse than that, I didn't feel welcome at the University of East London.

As at many universities, UEL students and staff were very politically active. University life seemed full of demos and protests, fighting the system, fighting the government, shouting about inequality, them and us, rich and poor, good and bad. This climate of constant conflict and resistance seemed so far from all I had been searching for. I remember one trip to an anti-racism meeting, where I heard more spitting bile and hatred than I might from a group of neo-Nazis.

41

It was while studying anthropology at UEL that I first read Victor Turner. He introduced me to the strange, slightly mystical notion of 'communitas'. It is a difficult concept to capture in a few words, but it is something along the lines of 'collective joy'. A feeling of togetherness, oneness, and equality that bubbles up amongst people sharing a common purpose. Communitas sounded like everything I had been looking for.

I may have studied communitas at UEL, but I experienced alienation and loneliness. I mean, I was *researching* communitas for goodness' sake! Why couldn't I feel it? In desperation, I joined the university samba band and played a few gigs. I attended the department's summer solstice camp, close to Avebury stone circle. But I always felt like an outsider, like someone who could never quite break through into the cliques.

I was becoming more and more isolated, like a satellite, looking in at the world. I'd often visit Brighton to see Robin and my best friend, Nadja, for a day. But my drive back to London was always filled with dread, my mood dropping as I reached the outskirts of the city.

While in London I began a brief and impossibly stormy relationship with a completely unsuitable older man. Let's call him Stefan. Stefan was German, and for a while I found the foreignness rather exotic and exciting. He was also protective of me, dominating, wealthy and clever. He allowed me to let go of trying to control things, just a little, and act like a little girl. I felt safe and looked-after, and it was the first time since my dad's death that I had something approaching a father figure. But Stefan was a very solemn chap who thought the whole world was his business to have an opinion about. And before long, I became stifled by Stefan's intensity and seriousness, and I think he was probably irritated by my silliness. The rows were savage. I would eventually come out of that relationship almost mentally destabilised. If there is such a thing as a soul mate, perhaps there is also such a thing as a soul enemy. I often used to wonder if Stefan and I were soul enemies.

In my daydreams, I'd think about my ideal man. I imagined him exactly, with blue eyes and dark hair. He'd be broad across the chest, chunky rather than slim, with a cracking sense of humour, never taking life very seriously. He'd also be passionate and sexy. He'd be calm, tolerant, and politically similar to me. And he'd love cats.

I may have hated living in London, but I did love Walthamstow Village. Little more than one street, Walthamstow Village was a small part of the desperately poor Waltham Forest area of East London. It was there that I asked for a job in a pub in the village, the Nag's Head. I didn't need the money, I simply wanted the company of ordinary people and a break from the incessant political tension of university life.

Working at the Nag's Head was one of the highlights of my years in London. Spending my evenings with a bunch of working-class London barmaids, I had some of the funnest and funniest nights of my life. Two of the women in particular, Jade and Vanessa, had the power to make me laugh out loud. The landlady, Flossie, and the landlord, Roger, were true Londoners who wouldn't seem out of place in a Dickens novel. In that little sanctuary, I felt genuinely happy a lot of the time. Sometimes, amongst the bustle and noise, a Glimpse would well up in me, filling me with bliss. It was not in studying ancient societies that I found a few brief moments of communitas, it was there, in that little pub full of ordinary East End Londoners.

One Friday evening when I was working in the Nag's Head, a man walked up to the bar. He had blue eyes, dark hair with flecks of grey, and a big smile already on his face. He was broad across the chest, chunky rather than slim. My heart skipped as I looked up into his eyes. He looked back with a similar startled look as if to say, 'Do I know you?'

Whoa! What a rush. What was *that* about?

I couldn't tell you why I found him so attractive, but I'd never felt a pull so strong. It was like something woke up within me, a warmth, an excitement. The attraction was apparently mutual because we spent the rest of the evening glancing across at each other, he with a cheeky grin, me looking shyly away like Princess Diana.

And so began the long, slow flirtation. Every Friday he would come in, with a bunch of friends, and we would watch each other across the bar. One evening, I decided it was time we spoke. Like a schoolgirl, I sent my friend Jodi to ask three questions:

What's your name?

How old are you?

What do you do?

I discovered his name was Mike, he was 36, and he was a photographer. (In my previous books, I called him 'Robert'.) When my shift ended, we sat at one of the small pub tables and spoke for the first time. Alas, he was not single. He had recently started a relationship and wanted to see how it went before starting anything new. And I had to admit, I was no more single than he was, still embroiled in the tumultuous relationship with Stefan. I was never one for cheating, and neither, it seemed, was he. The night ended. And that was that. The very next day, my shifts at the pub changed. I was sent to work in the sister pub of the Nag's Head, an establishment called The Castle, and I never saw The Beautiful Mike in the Nag's Head ever again.

Within a few months, my German and I split for the last time. We separated with surprisingly little animosity. Stefan must have felt as relieved as I that that horrible relationship was over and that we were both free to find mates more suited to our wildly different dispositions. I haven't spoken to him since. I do hope he is happy.

For months I watched for The Beautiful Mike to come back into the pub, but he never did. Frustratingly, he had come in on a few of my days off and had even asked after me. But no numbers had been left. No means of contact was possible.

How is it possible to have that level of attraction between two people and have nothing come of it? I had put an intention into the world designed to manifest an exact person, and then, when that person appeared he promptly disappeared without a trace.

Having split with Stefan, I felt more alone than ever. My divorce had come through, and I was rapidly spending through the settlement (arranged privately between my ex-husband and me prior to divorcing) I received when we'd sold our house.

After two years in London, I was coming to realise how just little I fit in around there. I'd gone to UEL looking for belonging, for togetherness, merriment and community. But for some reason, I was eyed with suspicion and only ever felt grudgingly tolerated. At UEL I had discovered the perfect *concept* of communitas, but most of the time, I was light years away from experiencing it.

My PhD supervisors were committed revolutionaries. For a while, this way of thinking had seemed to rub off on me. I even attended a few demos, but it wouldn't stick. I was never going to be one of them, and more and more, I came to sense I was being forced to write a thesis based more on political ideology than the evidence I saw.

The final straw came on the day my purse was snatched on Walthamstow High Street. I was heartbroken, not over the money I had lost, which was only a few pounds, but over the loss of the purse (bought as a present by a seven-year-old Robin) and a scrap of paper inside it. On that bit of paper, in my ex-husband's writing, was a recipe for the best ever apple and blackberry crumble.

The decision was made that day. I couldn't stand it a second longer. I didn't belong at UEL. I didn't belong at Avebury camp. I didn't belong in the samba band. And I certainly didn't belong in London. I couldn't make it in London. I couldn't live there. I was going back to Brighton, to Robin, to my mother, to Nadja. To friendly, safe Brighton with its clean sea air, its cafés full of dogs and its smiling bus drivers.

6. Back in the Real World

I had now failed not one, not two, but *three* PhDs. Despite everything, giving up on that final doctorate was one decision I have often regretted. It was when I decisively, absolutely left that third — and last — university that everything fell apart.

One good thing did come out of my time in London — I got over my insomnia. It was not doctors or therapists, but self-help books that had eventually allowed me to beat that debililtating affliction once and for all. And, without the excuse of insomnia, I was ready to enter the real world — the world of working for a living.

That was when I discovered what a sheltered and unreal existence academia had been for me. I had managed to leave 15 years at university with no knowledge of how to do anything other than write a half-decent essay and teach basic philosophy to first-year undergrads. Try going into a job interview with those sorts of qualifications! The 'real' jobs required experience, skills, knowledge of software packages and work practices. I didn't even understand the jargon they used. (To this day, I don't understand what a database, a project manager, or a systems analyst actually does.) In interviews for lower paid jobs, they'd take one look at my academic record and deem me overqualified. I was stuck. Stuck and getting dangerously close to middle age.

By that time, I had written and released my first book (more details on that later) and built a clumsy, clunky website to promote it. But the book was not earning anything like enough money to keep me alive, and I was having to spend almost every penny of the royalties on ongoing promotion, publicity and maintaining the website. For months, I worked full-time to publicise the book, trying every promotional activity there was. But I couldn't afford to pay top professionals to help with the very technical aspects of my business. Every time I paid an apparent professional to help me with websites, SEO (search engine optimization), marketing, or anything web-based, I'd find the cheapest on the market. I soon discovered that when you pay peanuts, you very often get monkeys.

Consequently, I learned to do everything myself: SEO, copywriting, website building and design. I edited and formatted my book myself. But everything looked shoddy and half-arsed. I may have been a jack of all trades, but I was master of absolutely nothing. I made a lot of expensive mistakes, spent all my divorce settlement, ran up mountains of debt, and paid for appalling service after appalling service. While the sales were okay, and reviews were great, it sometimes felt that book was more of a money pit than anything else.

At this stage, I was still angry, complaining and bitter, and readers could hear it coming off the pages of my book. I may have been helping people, but my bedside manner left something to be desired. Most of the unfavourable reviews for my first book were from people telling me I was bossy, dogmatic, arrogant, opinionated.

They were right.

Finally, I managed to bag a job. It was for minimum wage factory work, packing CDs. Even then, the manager who hired me was reluctant to take me on after looking at my academic record. She flat-out told me I was overqualified for the job. I only convinced her to hire me by laying on quite a sob story about the state of my debts. I told her I had bills to pay, that my book sales weren't enough to live on, that I couldn't afford the time to retrain — in short, I told her the truth. She believed me, and at last, I had a job.

I was the wrong side of 40, with three failed PhDs. I was single, overweight, in debt, and about to start a mindless minimum wage job, just to keep bankruptcy and eviction at bay.

And so, we come full circle. We come back to Genevieve, working in the factory, with her clapped-out Ford Ka standing outside her crummy flat. Let's rejoin her, shall we, asleep in front of the television, a microwave meal in her tummy.

7. I May Never Make It

When I woke up in the morning after I fell asleep in front of the television, a horrible realisation started to dawn on me. I'd like to show you my journal entry for the day,

I may never make it.

After all, I am now 43. If it hasn't happened yet, it probably never will. Perhaps this is it. Perhaps this is as good as it gets.

I have officially hit financial rock-bottom. I have never been in as bad a financial mess as I am now. I owe £32k on credit cards and am about to go over my extra, special, emergency reserve overdraft fund. That is, £500 on top of the £2600 overdraft I have had at full capacity for years. That's £35,000 of debt.

Something has to change, fast. Either I need some success from my book, or I need to go and get a proper job and spend the next ten years slogging it out just to pay off my debts. I am genuinely frightened that I could end up bankrupt.

It was that Sunday when it happened. It was around five in the afternoon, and I was washing my work clothes, getting everything ready for my shift in the morning. The start of a new work week. And it came to me: I had spent the whole weekend without seeing another living soul.

I was working to survive. I was working to eat. I was working to pay off my debts. But other than that, I had no life at all. I had very few friends, no boyfriend, no money and no hope. The only good things in my life were Robin and my one best friend, Nadja. I hated everything else in my life. I was bored, anxious and depressed. Can you be bored and anxious and depressed all at the same time? Well, apparently you can, because I was all three at that moment. That day I felt so utterly lost, so hopeless. My stomach felt like it contained a lead weight, dragging me down, giving me a permanently sinking sensation.

Something is very wrong.
Something is very wrong.

It was my spontaneously occurring mantra.

How had my life become this? How had I lost all joy and the ability to have fun? The thought hit me that I literally did not know how to be happy anymore. In fact, I couldn't even really remember what happy felt like.

With that, I literally collapsed in despair. On my knees, I remember catching sight of the badly laid floor of my tiny one-bedroomed flat — a floor I had never been able to afford to carpet. Fake wood veneer strips covered it. I don't mean it was covered with fake wood. It was covered in fake veneer — one step down from *actual* veneer. These strips were made of plastic, with an inkjet wood-effect image, attached directly to the concrete floor with glue. They were nothing more than plastic, floorboard-shaped stickers.

Without the insulation of underlay, the floor was always freezing cold and rock hard.

Whoever had lived in the house before me had laid the strips butted up, aligned next to each other like soldiers, not staggered like bricks. The floor was laid as if by a toddler building Lego chimneys, putting one block directly on top of another. Even children eventually come to realise Lego must be staggered, but it had not apparently occurred to the layer of this floor. They hadn't even lined them up neatly; there were gaps everywhere.

Somehow, the sight of that horrible floor struck me like never before. I was 43 and didn't know when I would ever have the money to carpet over that awful job. I was ashamed of the floor, ashamed of my home, and desperately ashamed of myself. It was one of the lowest moments of my life.

Why can't someone *help me?* I thought. *Please, someone, anyone, help me!*

I'd only once in my life felt that desperate before, and that was in the depths of a particularly dreadful spate of missed nights of sleep, at the height of my insomnia problem. I remember screaming at God to help me and then going out into the streets to search for a heroin dealer. (I had heard that heroin gives the most delicious, ecstatic sleep.) But I had no idea how to buy that sort of drug. I didn't move in circles where heroin was available, thank goodness. And so, I never did take it, but it's incredible the things desperation will lead you to consider.

And there I was again, asking for help, looking for the answer

When suffering from insomnia, I'd had to tackle the problem myself. No doctor had had the answer. No one had come to help me when I had demanded it. No one had turned up when I had yelled out in the sleepless nights. No one had listened to my raging, to my begging, to my praying. Utterly alone and isolated in the misery of insomnia, I'd had to turn to *self-help*. I had overcome my sleep problems by looking at my own life and by taking steps to change it. With no one else to turn to, I'd had no choice.

And now, years later, sitting there on the stick-on, fake veneer floor, I felt that same sense of isolation once again. No one was coming. No one was listening. No one would save me. I had already been forgotten.

PART 2
BECOMING
GENEVIEVE

8. No One Came

I picked myself up off the floor, suddenly awake to a fresh new thought: no one was coming.

I realised the enormity of the insight I had just had.

No one was coming.
No one was coming.
No one was coming.

No one would help me. Family, friends, doctors, therapists, society, the government — *were not going to help me.* It was down to me.

But rather than depressing me further, this thought seemed to wake me up out of my misery. It was as if breaking down and giving up had allowed something to break free. In the release of utter despair, the black churning thoughts had settled, stopped. This allowed a fresh, new thought to bubble up and escape — *an insight.*

It had *always* been down to me. All of it. It had never been for someone else to fix. Nothing would change unless I did this for myself. At that moment, a sense of enormous empowerment overtook me.

I could do this myself.

I didn't have to wait anymore. I didn't have to be angry at doctors or society, or my upbringing, or anyone else. I didn't have to live in bitter blame. I didn't have to allow my life to be ruled by the inaction of others. It really was *all about me*.

And it felt good!

I felt more alive than I had in years. From that place, I had fresh eyes to see everything anew. I looked back at my life and saw how much I had blamed everyone and everything for my lot in life. I could see how I had lost the power and magic of childhood and how much of a victim I had become.

My life was no one's responsibility but mine.

Suddenly, taking responsibility was not scary. It was not too much to stand. It was not overwhelming. It was control. True control over my life.

The best part was that it meant I didn't have to wait a second longer for my life to start. I could begin changing things, *right at that moment*. And if things went wrong, I didn't have to get angry at someone. I didn't have to blame someone and wait for them to put it right. If I got things wrong, I'd just do something else.

If you've read any of my books on magic, you'll know that I make quite a song and dance about *taking responsibility*. Even if you don't believe a single word of what I say about magic, consider this: taking responsibility is the most powerful thing you can ever do. This point is often misunderstood as victim-blaming. Blaming the victim? Do me a favour! Taking responsibility is the direct *opposite* of victimhood. Victimhood implies powerlessness. The very definition of a victim is someone at the wrong end of a power imbalance. But one of the greatest things about taking responsibility is that it makes you *powerful!* When you take responsibility, you don't end up sitting around waiting for someone to fix things. You don't have to get angry at someone else whose job it should be to sort things out. You don't have to endure their neglect or negligence anymore. It's all down to you. Your rules. Your timeframe.

Taking responsibility has nothing to do with whose fault things are or about who caused things to go wrong in the first place. Someone else may well have caused the problem, but it's still for you to sort it. Taking responsibility is about doing what you can with the hand you've been dealt.

Enough was enough. I would draw a line in the sand. I made a written commitment, much like the one I ask readers to make in *Becoming Magic*. These are the words I wrote:

From this day forward, I (insert real name here), commit to taking responsibility for my life. Overcoming my sleep problem was not the responsibility of anyone else. It was not up to doctors to find a cure. No, it was up to me. It can be the same with all aspects of my life. It is not up to someone else to fix my life. From now on, I will take my future into my own hands.

I will become great

And I will create an exceptional life for myself.

I wrote these words down on a piece of paper, and I signed it. I used the paper as a bookmark for years, and I still have it somewhere.

From that day on, nothing would be the same again.

Warning:

The following section details my discovery of using magic to manifest stuff in my life. My thinking has now changed somewhat. However, this doesn't negate the truth of how it seemed to me given my understanding at that time. I leave the story intact, as a narrative, but *not* as a template for you to do your own magic. Do not take my experience as a precise set of instructions.

In fact, be very, very suspicious of anyone offering precise instructions for anything other than assembling Ikea furniture

9. My Thoughts Returned to Magic

In those murky first days, I was open to all possibilities, and I found my mind wandering back to childhood, when I'd seemed able to get anything I wanted, like magic. How had I lost that ability?

If only I could still do magic, I thought.

I remembered my pagan friend Jo, and what she had said about magic. At the time, I hadn't paid much attention, but now the words came back with sudden significance. 'A magic spell is just an intention', she had said. *Intention.* I remembered seeing a book called *The Power of Intention* by Wayne Dyer and my rejecting it as too woo-woo smelling. But now, my mind was open. There was no place in this desperate soul for bloody-mindedness and stubbornness. I didn't mind what it smelled of. If it helped me, I'd have read anything.

A quick search and Amazon came up with the goods. I bought *The Power of Intention* by Wayne Dyer. I also picked up *Think and Grow Rich* by Napoleon Hill and *The Secret* by Rhonda Byrne on DVD.

I was utterly transfixed by Napoleon Hill's words. *Thoughts are things,* he said. I also watched *The Secret* and heard that not only are thoughts things, but thoughts *become* things. *Thoughts become things* was apparently governed by a mysterious law, the 'law of attraction', the idea that we attract everything in our lives with thought. If you didn't like your life, all you needed to do was change your thinking, moving your mind off what you *don't* want and on to what you *do* want. What a spectacularly exciting prospect!

It's easy to understand, well, the *attraction* of an idea like the law of attraction. What those books seemed to be telling me was that I didn't have to *do* anything to change my life; I just had to think the right thoughts. I just had to think hard about something I wanted and sit back and watch that thing manifest before my eyes. As Rhonda Byrne said:

Thoughts become *things*.

This was made doubly alluring by Rhonda's suggestion that knowledge of the law of attraction and of *thoughts become things* is a big *Secret*, kept from ordinary people. There had been a conspiracy of silence surrounding how the world really worked, kept from the likes of us for centuries by a group of Illuminati-style rich and powerful men.

How exciting is *that*?

Yes, yes, yes, of course, the whole notion of manifesting stuff out of thin air seemed ridiculous, particularly for someone who had spent years studying analytic philosophy. But there appeared to be some pretty respectable people who believed in this stuff, so I owed it to them to consider it with some seriousness.

Nope... that's not true. I'm making that bit up.

It had nothing to do with the opinions of respectable people. That's simply me post-rationalising. The real reason I entertained the idea of manifesting was far less reasonable. I entertained the notion of a law of attraction because I was *desperate*. And desperation can lead a person to consider all sorts of irrational things.

And I suspect, despite protestations to the contrary, and despite claiming to be 100% scientific, rational and atheistic, in the dark recesses of our own private beliefs, many of us harbour and entertain some profoundly irrational notions. And let's face it, wouldn't it be amazing if the law of attraction were even slightly real? If it didn't work, the worst that would happen was nothing. If it did work, well, my life was sorted. And it wasn't like I had to tell anyone about my crazy plan. So, it was totally in secret that I set about testing the process of manifesting *things* with *thought*.

At first, it was all about the money. Because the shifts at the factory were 12 hours long, it meant I was able to rack up 60 to 70 hours a week. And even at minimum wage, 70 hours' work meant enough money to survive while also keeping up with my five huge credit card payments. But the entire £32k debt was accruing interest at the brutal standard credit card rate. I was maxed out. There were great 0% offers everywhere, but I couldn't take advantage of them. Because my debt was so large, no one would give me a new card to which to transfer any of it.

I remember the payment on my Halifax card was £160 per month. But only £5 of that £160 went to paying off the debt. The remaining £155 was interest. At that rate, it would take me *60 years* to pay off that one debt. Sixty years! I wouldn't live that long!

Something needed to change. And, just maybe, the art of manifesting would be the answer.

My first, floundering attempts at manifesting were all of the same sort. Pretty standard stuff for a brand new manifestor — trying to attract a billion pounds. After all, I reasoned, I needed something *big* to happen, something huge. It would be no good only manifesting the £32k required to pay off my debts. I needed enough money to change my life, get me out of that factory, start again.

Plus, I kept on reading the same message — *The universe doesn't mind whether you ask for a billion pounds or a penny; it's all the same to the universe. It's just as easy for it to send you a large amount of money, so you might as well ask for the billion.*

So I set out to win, not the UK National Lottery with its paltry £3m prize but the huge EuroMillions jackpot that often rolled over to a 50, 70, or 100-million-euro jackpot. As this was my only chance of changing my life, I reasoned, I might as well put all my energy into trying to win it.

Decades earlier, I had watched an episode of a UK soap called *Brookside*, in which one of the characters won the UK lottery by following a certain mathematical system. After a bit of research, I discovered it was possible to stack the odds ever so slightly in your favour by following certain rules. For example, did you know that very often a number from the weekly draw will be repeated the following week? Or that that the number 46 is the least often drawn number in the UK National Lottery? Or that by 'wheeling' numbers (playing all the possible combinations of a larger set of numbers), you can increase the statistical chances of winning quite considerably?

I bought an online lottery-winning program called Smart Luck, created by an American woman called Gail Howard. This program automated things so that I didn't have to do the calculations myself, and I would spend every Sunday poring over her program, studying and scrutinising the previous winners so I could pick the perfect set of statistically likely numbers.

Right. That was the science stuff sorted. Now for the manifesting part.

Following the advice of Napoleon Hill and Rhonda Byrne to keep my mind on thoughts of my desire, I flooded my mind with thoughts about winning the lottery. I left Post-it notes all over the house and did hundreds and hundreds of affirmations, all attesting to my imminent millionaire status. I visualised myself winning, over and over. I visualised while meditating. I visualised while exercising. I even planned the way I would react when I heard the news I had won and how I would spend the remainder of that special day. I had it clear and so crisp and precise in my mind, I could almost taste it. I was doing everything right. I just *had* to win.

But week after week went by without picking even a single number correctly.

Undeterred, I bought book after book on the law of attraction. I read every internet article. I watched every YouTube video. I was particularly thrilled by the story of John Assaraf. John had manifested his ideal dream house after sticking a photo of it to a vision board. The very same house! Hugely inspired by this, I bought a thick sheet of MDF (kind of like particleboard) from the DIY shop. After a lovely day of cutting and sticking, my vision board was complete. In the main, it was covered with pictures of banknotes. (There were also a few Aston Martin DB7s.) Every day I looked at that vision board. It was the first thing I saw when I woke every morning.

More weeks went by, more lottery draws were held, but the universe very stubbornly *refused to pay up*.

I kept reading that by focusing on something for at least 17 seconds, you start to manifest that thing in the world. That whatever you hold in your mind for long enough has to come to you. And because this is true, you cannot allow yourself the luxury of a negative thought.

So *that* was the issue — it was my sneaky destructive thinking that did it. I was sabotaging my manifestations by letting too many negative thoughts pop in. I needed to keep thinking lovely thoughts and to stop thinking about bad things. I began actively and frantically monitoring my thoughts, trying to force myself to think of nothing but love and kittens and unicorns.

Have you ever tried this? Have you ever tried keeping your thoughts on only positive things? Have you ever tried keeping your mind on only what you want, and off those things you don't? It's flipping impossible! (Not only that, I've since discovered it's *literally* impossible.)

I can't remember whose advice it was to take your dream car for a test drive, to get used to the feeling of the leather steering wheel on your hands, to feel like a millionaire. It wasn't only about thinking, it was also about feeling too. Now I had the answer — make it feel so real that it has no choice but to burst into reality.

So I did this. I took an Aston Martin for a test drive. It wasn't even a brand new one (I wasn't nearly confident enough to do that). I looked through AutoTrader and found that a local garage had a second-hand DB9 for sale. I remember it had a £49,000 price tag — not even that expensive by today's standards. But it was way out of my league, having been used to driving a beaten-up Ford Ka with no MOT and a cracked windscreen. My Ford Ka was worth about £600, and there I was test-driving a £49,000 car. When I turned up to the garage to drive the car, I felt sick and totally overwhelmed by the whole situation. It must have been screamingly obvious I wasn't a serious buyer. I was merely a time waster, a tyre-kicker. And, after being treated with disdain by the salesman, I left utterly despondent, ridiculous and humiliated.

So much for that little gem of advice.

But, the brown cardboard Amazon book boxes were still landing on my doormat. Every Sunday I'd read a new book and get excited all over again. I thought surely things would change when I discovered the first proponents of New Thought — a whole movement dedicated to the business of manifesting. New Thought was akin to a religion and had many clever and worthy advocates. These people would surely know the truth. They would know how and if this stuff really worked.

The most compelling of the New Thought books was *The Master Key System* by Charles Haanel. Unlike many other writers, Haanel didn't pretend this manifesting process was easy. *The Master Key System* was a 24-part study course, designed to be spread over six months. This guy was serious, and I was thrilled. If anything was going to work, it was surely this!

The Master Key System quickly became my bible. I did the exercises in it, one at a time, practised the visualisations, and read and re-read the text. I followed the instructions to the letter.

And nothing happened. *Nothing at all.*

You know, all the time I had worked on *The Master Key System*, vision boards, visualisation, affirmations and the like, a vital question had been nagging away at me — *Why did nothing of what these books were telling me fit my actual experience of life?*

For example, no matter how long I spent thinking about what I wanted, it never seemed to materialise. Whereas, when *bad* things happened, they came utterly out of the blue and almost never when I had been thinking about them.

How was that possible? If the world reflects my thinking, why didn't I manifest horrible things whenever I had negative thoughts? Why weren't my absolute worst fears popping into reality all over the place, considering I worried a lot of the time? If anything, it seemed the opposite was true — quite often when I thought about the very worst-case scenario, things would tend to turn out far *better* than I expected. It simply didn't seem true that focussing on good things made good things happen. Neither did it seem that focussing on bad things made bad things happen.

I did wonder whether these writers were telling the truth about their ability to manifest things. Maybe this *was* a load of old nonsense. All of it. Had I been suckered in, just like all the other desperate people?

It should have been perfectly obvious why nothing was happening.

I was expecting a million pounds to fall into my lap, just because I had conjured up some pretty thoughts.

I was following the words of others, religiously, and then blaming them when things didn't work.

I was still waiting for someone to save me, still effectively sitting on my backside, waiting for my life to start.

I may have been having loving thoughts of angels and lottery wins, but the rest of the time, I was still whining that I wasn't paid enough, that the minimum wage should be higher, that politicians earned too much, and that nurses earned too little. After all, I had never been properly appreciated. How could I be successful when there were attempts to thwart my efforts at every turn?

Many writers recommended feeling gratitude on a regular basis. Well, I'd feel gratitude when I had something to be grateful for, thank you very much. It's all very well feeling gratitude when you're a successful writer or speaker or guru. But try feeling grateful for your arsehole boss and your minimum wage job. Try feeling grateful when you don't even have carpet on your stick-on vinyl fake veneer floor. And what about those worse off than I was? What about those starving, with sick children, or with fatal diseases? Should they feel grateful too? The very suggestion was offensive.

And now, to add insult to injury, it turned out that those law of attraction writers were a bunch of charlatans! How *classic*. How typical of my crummy, disappointing life. This was how it was for me. This was my story. Life was very rudely ignoring me and my talents. If only the world would sit up, recognise my genius, and offer me a job more befitting my education and potential, *then* perhaps I would stop complaining. This is what I arrogantly believed at the time.

The truth was, I hadn't taken responsibility at all. I had merely *said* I had. And rather than work to sort my own life, there I was demanding that the universe hand me *millions* of pounds on a plate. Talk about a sense of entitlement! Talk about expecting handouts. Talk about not taking responsibility! Looking back now, I'm somewhat ashamed of myself.

I can pinpoint the exact point things began to change. I was in the park, reading a copy of *The Astonishing Power of Emotions* by Esther and Jerry Hicks. As I came to the part where the authors talked about 'turning the boat downstream', something happened. As I mentally turned my metaphorical boat downstream, a lightness came over me, like a release. A sort of contented, comfortable warmth. I felt a sense of letting go, as if I had slotted into the current of life rather than trying to force things to happen.

What's that about?

To my astonishment, the feeling was *gratitude.* Nothing in my life had changed. I was still poor, I was still lonely, but there I was feeling gratitude for the sense of 'okayness' that was flooding over me. And it felt *good.*

In an instant, I completely understood the fuss made about gratitude. I could see all the people and circumstances I was blaming for my misfortune. And I thought, *They can't feel your anger. They can't hear your grumbling.* And, what's more, *Your feeling gratitude doesn't touch them.*

Gratitude wasn't about acknowledging there are people worse off than I was. It was not that I *should* have felt grateful, given my circumstances. This was not about guilt or obligation.

The only one who could feel my gratitude was me.

The good feeling stayed with me and I had the smoothest, happiest Sunday simply by turning my boat downstream, feeling a little gratitude and realising that, right at that moment, everything was actually okay. What a difference it would make to feel like that on a more regular basis!

But it was getting late. I had to be up at 5 am and start a new week at work. I was dreading it. I couldn't stand the thought of those miserable, blank faces, of having to stand for 12 hours until my back ached and my feet were singing in pain. Right then, there was nothing more I wanted than not to have to go to work in the morning. I began to fantasise about a bomb dropping on the factory. I even considered 'throwing a sickie' just so I could stay home. But rather than fretting until bedtime and spoiling what was left of my evening, I did something else. Once again, I metaphorically turned my boat downstream and felt the associated release. The soft, safe, comfortable sensation came over me once again. Perhaps work wouldn't be so bad after all.

Right then, my mobile phone pinged a message. It was work. *Due to a supplier problem, production has been halted for 24 hours. There will be no work tomorrow.* I was astonished. Had I manifested something? Something had actually happened. Something that went beyond the usual pepped-up feeling I got from reading self-help books. And all I had done was 'turn my boat downstream'.

As the days went on, I noticed that whenever I turned the boat downstream, I'd fall into that good-feeling place. Life would appear to pick up and small things would go my way. So now, I had one small thing I could do that appeared to make things a teeny bit better. I wasn't exactly manifesting my millions, but at least things weren't going to hell anymore.

Because of experiences like this, I gave up on the notion of a 'law of attraction', no matter what the books said to the contrary. I also gave up on Napoleon Hill's suggestion that it was essential to feel 'burning desire' for your goal in order for it to be attracted to you. In fact, I started to notice something very different. It's something that many of us have experienced. More than once, the object of my desire would suddenly appear in my life after I had stopped asking for it, had stopped wanting it, or had forgotten I had ever asked for it in the first place. It was as if the wanting and asking had kept my goal at bay. Far from attracting the things I wanted, it seemed more like 'burning desire' worked effectively to keep them away from me.

The books were all saying one thing. But my experience was telling me something quite different.

The Snap-Backs

I came home from work one evening to find a letter waiting for me. In it was a cheque for £438. Completely out of the blue, I had received a tax rebate. Relaxing on the sofa, I picked up my journal and wrote, 'Hallelujah! It's starting to work!' I'd finally have enough to MOT my car.

When I looked up from my journal, I noticed my elderly cat, Chipper, wasn't looking happy. Usually such a cheerful soul, he was sitting with his eyes scrunched closed, and when I touched him, his body felt tense and hard, not soft and squidgy like a cat should. I gave him a piece of tuna as a treat, but when he tried to eat it, he howled in pain.

The emergency vet discovered many of his teeth were rotten, and some were almost falling out. Poor Chipper came back from the vet six teeth lighter.

I came back £430 lighter. Almost every penny of my manifested money was gone.

Then it happened again. One day, I discovered the SEO strategies I had been working on for months had paid off. The clumsy little website that promoted my book had risen to the number 1 spot on Google for all sorts of high-traffic keywords. Sales were flooding in. I remember being so happy that I wasn't going to be poor anymore. Things were going to change. Everything was going to be okay.

A few days later, I noticed my sales were down. Checking online, I discovered my search listings had vanished. I wasn't on page one, two, three, or *anywhere*. Traffic was down to a trickle. What was going on? A quick web search on 'my search listings have disappeared' explained the issue. I had fallen victim to the notorious Penguin update. Google had changed its algorithm, deciding that all the previous SEO techniques were no longer acceptable. In the space of a couple of days, my website had become virtually invisible. My hard work had been for nothing. I would have to start over again. It was heartbreaking. It was the cruelty of the taking away after coming so close that stung the most. I was on the brink of success, and it had been snatched away. Again.

Those early manifestation attempts were hard to bear. I didn't know what was worse — manifesting nothing or manifesting something amazing, only to see it vanish before my eyes. Why give me something I wanted so badly, only to snatch it off me? Why offer me The Beautiful Mike and then take him away? Why give me page one of Google and then send me tumbling down the listings? Why give me a tax rebate and then wipe it out with a vet bill? I had become able to manifest things, it seemed, but they would inevitably leave me.

I came to call these 'snap-backs'.

It was these snap-backs that convinced me that something was happening. Things weren't happening in the way the law of attraction books claimed they would, but *something* was happening. My attempts at manifestation didn't have the desired effect, but they did have *some* effect. They didn't do *nothing*. Now, I *knew* manifesting wasn't all nonsense. I had seen too many odd things working too many times to reject this as utter rubbish. *Something* was going on, and I wanted to know what.

Who could give me the answer? I'd read every book out there, and I just didn't know whom to trust.

10. Where Was My Guru?

I needed a teacher. Someone to talk to about what was happening, someone to defer to, someone to tell me if it was true, someone to *tell me what to do*. I'd always wanted to find a wise person, a guru — even a cult leader would do — to follow and worship and idolise and learn about. *When the student is ready, the master will appear*, so the saying goes. (And he will usually appear in yoga pants, with a long beard and a deeply lined ancient face with oh-so-youthful sparkly eyes.)

I had read *The Alchemist, The Monk Who Sold His Ferrari*, and *The Celestine Prophecy*, and the story was always similar. A man (usually a man) goes off to India or climbs a mountain and meets a mystical teacher (usually another man) who somehow knows the answers to everything. This teacher takes him on a journey of discovery, despite the author's stubborn protestations and childish resistance. But the teacher, with Christ-like patience, merely smiles and rewords his questions, using an almost Socratic and faintly patronising method to lead the author where he needs to go.

I was ready. I was *so* ready for my teacher. Sooner or later, he would appear to teach me and lead me to the life I deserved. Only it didn't happen. I waited and waited, and nobody came.

Go to India, I kept hearing. *All the best teachers come from India. India is the most wonderfully spiritual place. That's where you'll find your teacher.*

But I had no urge whatsoever to go to India. I didn't want to put a bindi on my head and change my name to something that sounded more exotic. By the way, it's not that I have anything against people who want to do that, in fact, I was envious of anyone having an experience so profound they feel compelled to change their name. But this whole Eastern business didn't 'speak to me'. It merely felt alien, foreign, even a smidge contrived. It certainly didn't feel magical. And while some people get something special from this sense of differentness, I didn't. It simply didn't resonate.

But I did feel magic right at home, in the green and damp and drizzly rain of the British Isles. After all, it was only here that I experienced *The Glimpse,* that flash of something magical, a remembrance of a fantastical otherworld that was, at the same time, *so* familiar. I felt it most strongly in old buildings, standing amid stone hut circles on Dartmoor, listening to the wind whistle across the South Downs, and on Christmas Eve. Sometimes I felt a Glimpse at other not-so-obvious times too, like when I'm playing Bioshock, seeing the femininity in a woman, really *seeing* it... and you know that bit at the end of the first Lord of the Rings film when Frodo (Elijah Wood) is holding the ring in the palm of his hand, before he jumps in the boat to run away from Sam? Well, I almost always have a Glimpse then too.

So how was India going to help me? I wanted a home-grown spirituality. And part of me always wondered why magic and spirituality *should* be limited to the East. Are we too stupid, ignorant or closed-minded in the West to generate any enlightened teachers? Don't we do ourselves a disservice by thinking we have to run off halfway around the world to learn anything remotely significant?

If India does it for you, that's fantastic. After all, I know many people are incredibly drawn to visit, and often people have hugely transformative experiences while there.

But what about those of us who don't?

I wanted to tell the story of an ordinary British woman, wearing jeans and make-up, drinking too much coffee, eating too many carbs, and not recycling enough. She doesn't find spirituality on an Indian mountain. She finds it here, in her own society full of cars and buses and commuters and iPads and computer games and 24-hour news channels. And if it is possible to find magic *here*, it is possible anywhere.

No, my teacher needed to be close to home.

And then I realised... I already knew my teacher.

No one was coming.

No one would turn up to help.

I had to do this for myself.

And my teacher was *me*.

I realised I'd had enough of following someone else's teachings and blaming them for my misfortune when they didn't work. It was time to look at what *did* work, for *me*. Rather than reading any more books, rather than searching online for the answers to my questions, I turned to the integrity of my own experience.

11. How the Magic Words
First Came to Me

It was back around the year 2006, while still married, that I first discovered I could write.

I had been sitting in the conservatory of the home I shared with my husband, writing in an A4 hardback book. We had an old park bench in the conservatory, and my beloved Siamese cat, Chipper, was curled up next to me. I had dropped into a place that felt great, where ideas were flowing, tumbling faster than I could keep up. I remember the words pouring out of me onto the paper like they were coming from another place, another voice. Those words would eventually become part of my first ever published book.

And then, years later, working in the factory, and living in a minuscule, grubby flat, my life having fallen apart, and having committed to changing my life, I found my mind going back to writing that first book. I remembered how good it had felt to feel those words flowing 'through' me onto the page. I remembered how effortless it had felt, like I had accessed a great source of wisdom, a voice that had spoken those words onto the paper. I was under no illusion that I was channelling spirits or anything remotely mystical. I just felt that I had tapped into a good place inside my own mind.

One Sunday morning, on my one day off from the factory, I decided to attempt to find that voice again, to access whatever I had found all those years ago, to discover what it had to say. I went early to the Costa Coffee above Tesco's in Hove. I sat with my laptop. Just sat. I decided to let the voice speak, let it out. Let it say whatever it wanted to.

I sat, and I waited.

At first, nothing much happened. But before very long, the words started to come. The voice began to speak and, as it spoke, my fingers began to tap away on the laptop keys. The words started to appear on the page.

Open your heart and listen, I typed.

Well, I wasn't expecting that. What in God's name did 'open your heart' mean? Did it mean to open up my chest with a scalpel to reveal the beating organ next to my lungs? No? So why not say what you mean?

And with a very *closed* heart, I carried on listening, having a mental conversation with the voice that was coming through onto the page. I would put up questions and objections and the voice would answer. And all the while, I carried on writing.

Do you remember as a child, you believed in magic? it said.

Well, yes, I did believe in magic. I believed in Father Christmas and the Tooth Fairy too. I was a child.

Do you remember as a child, you could do magic?

That one threw me. *Do* magic?

Do you remember the time that you could get anything you wanted, make things happen, affect the world around you? Do you remember when you were going to change the world, be a superstar, cure cancer, eradicate poverty, discover oil, marry a prince, and become the most famous person in the world?

Well, yes. I remembered feeling invincible and immortal. I remembered *knowing* that I was destined to have an exceptional life. I remember a time when I seemed able to say the word and get anything I wanted. But that was before I grew up, before life happened, before reality kicked in.

Where did that person go? Think back to your best Christmas ever. Hold onto that feeling and mix it with the first time you fell in love. What about the time you stood in a stone circle in Wessex and could feel the hum of the earth, the energy of history, the prickle of past generations standing there with you.

I felt the hair stand up on the back of my neck. A vast Glimpse had rushed through me. A light, flushing sensation came to my face. Then, as if I were in a Disney film, a beam of sunlight pierced the dimness of the clouds outside and lit the space where I sat. It was almost corny.

Then the voice said, *That's magic, that is.*

The world was suddenly alive. A rush of joy and peace washed over me. It was like being hugged by an angel. A flash of memory came to me, of childhood, that magical sense of being invincible and immortal you only really have under the age of 25. Glimpse followed Glimpse.

And then, I awoke to the energy around me. It was like tuning in to a noise that had been gently and imperceptibly humming in the background. The energy was soft, sweet but also exciting and gently electric. Like the hush and anticipation right before the curtain rises on a play. In that energy, I could *feel* the potential, as if, any moment, anything might happen. It was a breathless expectation. This went way beyond peace. This was approaching bliss.

And the voice carried on speaking. The words carried on coming. And I carried on writing…

Have you always had a lurking feeling you were meant for better things? Perhaps you feel you have some great talent, waiting to be discovered. Do you know you would be capable of so much more, if only you were given the opportunity? Do you go through life thinking life was not supposed to be this way, I am worth more than this, why are my talents not recognised? Or do you have a sense of longing, of searching for something you know not what? Do you feel that in some place, in another life, you would be shining like a diamond, rather than ignored and unnoticed as you are now, just another face in the crowd?

If you believe deep down that you are special, this is not some delusion; this reflects an underlying truth about you and the immensity of your true underlying power. I put it to you that you are still perfect, divine, and unbelievably powerful. Somewhere, deep down, your greatness is sitting … and waiting.

*You can begin to reawaken this magical, powerful part of you. If it has lain hidden for many years, there may be a lot of resistance to these instructions. If you are weak, you will give in to the force of argument that screams out to you that this is all nonsense. But if you are strong enough to let go and **trust**, without questioning every tiny thing, you may become more powerful than you ever dreamed.*

To this day, I don't remember thinking those words. I barely even remember writing them, such was the flow and speed at which they streamed out of me. There was no thought. There was no imagination at play. I didn't compose those words into existence. I didn't think them up. Just as it has always been with my very best writing, it was as if (and this really *stinks* of woo) they were coming to me from another place.

The words that came to me on that first day have barely changed from that day to this. They are the same words that, many years later, I used to begin my first book in the Course in Manifesting series, *Becoming Magic*. I gave them to you, just as they had come to me on that day, all those years before.

From that first day that the words came to me, there was a shift inside me.

I'd discovered magic. And it lived in *me.*

And finally, I'd discovered something about these Glimpses I've had since childhood. I learned that they weren't quite as elusive as I had imagined. They weren't far away at all. I didn't even need to go looking for them. They had been here all the time. They were in me, of me.

Why did I need to go halfway around the world, or even halfway across town to listen to a wise man? What would be the point? I had access to all the answers inside me. What greater source of wisdom was there than the truth of my own experience? I was not going to read one more word or listen to one more guru. There was only one consideration from now on:

What was true *for me?*

12. My First Experiment

I have always kept a journal. Since the age of 12 or 13, I have a record of all the high points and low points of life, written down in dozens of A4 hardback notebooks. And always, I have at least one small hardback notebook in my handbag to record any sudden insights, gratitude statements, or various other observations. I also have a large document on my computer I call my 'Book of Shadows'. For a long time, the words that spontaneously flowed from me were chronicled in that document.

I pulled up my Book of Shadows and the notes I had made over the years. This seemed the best place to start as, unlike anyone else's words, this was a faithful and accurate account of my own personal experiences. Unlike the books I had read, my Book of Shadows was *all* true *all* for me.

I went all the way back to the beginning, to the notes I had made when I first read *The Power of Intention* by Wayne Dyer. Wayne Dyer was just one big bundle of love. He recommended never harbouring a bad thought or saying a bad word about anyone, not complaining about people who cross you, but sending them love instead.

I had written in my journal two quotations from him.

Acceptance means no complaining, and happiness means no complaining about the things over which you can do nothing.

Loving people live in a loving world. Hostile people live in a hostile world. Same world. (That's one of my favourites.)

In other words, don't moan about corrupt politicians, send them love. Don't grumble about grumpy work colleagues, send them love. I had documented, at the time, the way life had seemed a little nicer when I followed his advice. But it had been merely an observation at the time, and I hadn't taken it very seriously.

Not complaining had always seemed an odd piece of advice to me. After all, how would anything change if you didn't complain? Wouldn't that turn me into some kind of doormat with people doing whatever the hell they liked, while I sat back and took it? That had generally been my reaction to that bit of wisdom. However, following my mystical experience in Costa Coffee, I was feeling less confrontational, and I was ready to try some of the more lovey-dovey advice with more dedication.

It was to be my first proper, conscious, well-documented experiment. I would try, for a period of two weeks, to avoid all complaining about life, or other people. I would refuse to see anything but good in anything that happened, even when what happened was upsetting, worrying or awful, even if I had to contrive to do so. And, most importantly, I would observe and record what happened *to* me and *for* me, when I did this.

That very next day, life at the factory seemed to pick up. I had the most enjoyable shift I'd had in months.

I could tell immediately that refusing to say mean things about other people was having a positive effect on *me*. I felt less tense, less churned up inside. When I thought kindly toward people who annoyed me, the tightness in my chest would drop with relief, like I'd let go of a weight, and when I let go of my irritation, the people around me seemed to react positively.

It was still dreadful work, and the hours were long and exhausting. But I also realised it was great to be amongst so many people. Rather than silently condemning my workmates for not laughing enough, for not smiling enough, I actively tried to see the good in them. In doing so, I opened up to their quiet Eastern European ways and came to understand them better. I learned that there is no such place as 'The Ukraine' (it is simply Ukraine), that there are dozens of Hungarian words for 'the joy felt at someone else's misfortune', and that there are still dragons living in Romania.

It's incredible how much connection you can feel when united under common hardship. People who had previously irritated the hell out of me became my friends, my comrades, my confidantes. We often had fun, chatting and trying to find ways to make the days go by with a little more interest and intrigue. I actually began to enjoy the job.

Previously, I had whinged incessantly about work because it was an awful job in an awful place for awful pay with awful people. Simply by not complaining, it had turned from awful to moderately enjoyable. All those years, I'd felt that complaining was the way to get things done, to change things for the better. It turned out, the opposite is true. Not complaining really had made the world a better place.

It was the birth of my 'no complaining' rule, one of the most powerful bits of advice I have ever offered. And it was this, the simple action of reducing my level of criticising and moaning that led me to that first major, life-changing insight about magic. It was during one of my Sunday mornings in Costa, after a long week at the factory, that the idea first came — I had improved my experience of life by merely telling a different story, by refusing to engage in bitching sessions.

I had changed me, and the world around me had changed.

It was a light bulb Eureka moment. *I was not ineffectual.* I was hugely, enormously powerful.

Let me explain.

You probably already know the basics of chaos theory: a butterfly's wings beating on one side of the earth can result in a hurricane on the other, etc., etc. Well, it's the same with a person. When you walk out into the world, no matter how unimportant or irrelevant you consider yourself, you are causing things to happen. The persona you put out into the world — the whole package of body, mind, feelings, actions, personality — is not a discrete lump of flesh moving in isolation through an unfeeling and uncaring universe. You may feel like a neglected and irrelevant bag of old clothes, unnoticed and unloved, but your very presence, whether you're happy or miserable, changes things. In simple terms, *you always have an effect.*

Thus, I could moan and bitch, I could drive like an inconsiderate so-and-so, I could swear at passers-by, I could be rude and sulky to everyone I met.

Or I could be pleasant and considerate, and people would react accordingly. By smiling at a stranger or helping an old lady carry her shopping, I was changing things, making history.

Even when I was doing nothing other than walking down the street with a smile on my face, *I had an effect.*

This idea blew my mind. I remember sitting and staring into space for hours, too astonished even to write. Because I realised *all of it* was in my control. I could control the me I put out into the world. And if I could change *me,* I could change the world.

I found that by behaving, speaking, looking a certain way at the factory, I could make the day go far better than usual. Even there, in that disempowered, underprivileged, exploited, minimum wage situation, *I still had an effect.*

It was not only what I was *doing,* or what I was *thinking,* but the way I was *being* that had shifted things. It was who I had *become* that made the difference. This was quite distinct from the old 'change your thoughts, change your life' advice. This was about *all of me,* the whole package, the way

I conducted myself. It was this that had the power to change things.

I wouldn't think *about* things I wanted, as the law of attraction books had advised. That had done *nothing*.

I would change *me*, choosing *who* to be, *how* to be, and watch as things changed around me.

I could become magic.

Once I knew this, it no longer made any sense to act the way I had been. If every little thing I did affected the world, I was going to make sure I made the best use of this enormous power. Some people are fond of asking, *'What would Jesus do?'* and then acting like that. I ask you to consider the person you would most like to be, imagine how they would dress, think, act, be. *What would she do? What would he do? Be like that.* I was going to be like the me who lived in my dreams. And as I did, my life took off with such velocity it was hard to keep up.

I had become magic. And when you become magic, you can *do* magic.

From this day on, right from this second, as you go out into the world, realise that you are *not* an insignificant dot in an uninterested and unforgiving universe. You are as powerful as any other human being on this planet. And I don't mean this in a cuddly, bigging-you-up, self-helpy way. I mean it literally. You are as powerful as Einstein or Mother Teresa or Mark Zuckerberg or Martin Luther King, Jr. Just by walking down the street, you have an effect. Just by passing the time of day with the waitress, you are having an effect. Just by stopping to let the other car pass where the road narrows, you are having an effect. Similarly, by letting your dog mess on the pavement, you are having an effect. By losing your temper with the bus driver, you are having an effect. By drinking a sneaky beer in your lunch break, you are having an effect.

I advise readers of *Becoming Magic* to write to me with their declaration to start a new life. Because when this realisation comes over *you*, when you realise the extent of your power to effect change in this world, something shifts, and life is never the same again.

13. Introducing the Receiving State

I came to see that there was a distinct *feeling* when I knew things were going my way. It seemed as if the *act* of taking responsibility, of feeling gratitude, of not complaining, of sending love to those who annoyed me allowed me to enter a particular state of being. I had first noticed this when I metaphorically turned my boat downstream, but now it became more and more familiar. It was a sense of wellbeing, a profound 'okayness', where everything looked brighter and more interesting. I'd feel alive, awake, and wanting for nothing. The longer and more often I achieved this state, the more things seemed to go my way, and because of this, I came to call it the *receiving state*.

This 'receiving state' seemed to sum up all the other good advice I had picked up. It was for me a kind of shorthand, an umbrella term. I could consciously stop complaining, feel gratitude, take inspired action… or I could enter the receiving state, and these things would happen automatically. That's how it seemed to me at the time.

The most obvious characteristic of the receiving state was *non-wanting*. I could *ask* for something incessantly, and nothing would ever happen. But when I moved away from asking for what I wanted, and into this state where I wanted for nothing, I would often receive exactly what I desired.

The receiving state felt rather like a slightly contrived version of *The Glimpse*. It wasn't as pure, as deep, as clean, as intense, as perfect as The Glimpse, but it was a pretty good second and, whereas the Glimpses came spontaneously, the receiving state seemed to be summonable at will. Other writers described 'letting go', 'surrender', 'getting out of the way', and I imagine they were talking about the same thing.

For me, the notion of *trust* worked every time.

I discovered the importance of trust one Christmas when my cat, Chipper, became very sick. He had done this before — fallen terribly ill and then perked up and carried on living for another year. Now, there I was again with a sick cat. I was in such a dilemma over whether to have him put to sleep or let him continue on for a little while. I was in an awful state, thinking one way and then the other, torturously trying to come up with a solution. Then, from somewhere, came the insight to just *trust*.

I stopped the wrangling. I stopped trying to work it out. I fell into trusting that everything was going to be okay, and a profound peace came over me.

Then another thought came to me:

You need to let him do some of the dying himself.

It's hard to explain why but for some reason, that was exactly what I needed to hear. I had been desperately trying to ensure my cat didn't suffer for one instant. But in doing so, I was denying his natural right to die in his own good time. A time might come when I would put him to sleep, and when that time came, I would have no doubts. But I wasn't there yet. So I asked my trusted vet, Andrew, to give my old pussycat anything he could to make him feel a little nicer. And, after a cortisone injection and some vitamin B12, I took Chipper home.

He perked up, recovered, and lived for *years!*

Eventually, my dear old cat did need the final injection from the vet. And when it happened, aged 19, lying on my lap in his own home, I had no doubt whatsoever that it was the right decision. (Blimey, writing this is bringing tears to my eyes, even though it was years ago!)

Trust had allowed me truly to let go trying to work out the answer. It had halted the thinking, judging, worrying, wanting. But this was something far more powerful than merely easing an overactive mind. When I made the decision to *trust*, utterly and completely, I accepted that everything, *everything* was working out just right. Trust allowed me to let go and stop trying to make things happen, to give up control and pass the reins to something greater, safe in the knowledge that everything was being taken care of for me.

Trust allowed me to drop into *the receiving state.*

Although I called it the *receiving* state, it didn't matter whether or not I ever received what I asked for, because I was trusting that no matter what did unfold it was precisely the right thing for me. It made no sense to be yearning after certain outcomes or worrying about things going wrong. When I trusted, I had no attachment to any particular outcome, not even to the thing I was attempting to create. And as a result, I almost always got exactly what I wanted.

The simple act of *trusting* somehow allowed me to do magic.

14. The Impossibly Serendipitous Joining of Guardian Soulmates

But what was I going to do to make a man happen into my life? I knew what I wanted in a potential mate. More than anything, I wanted cheerfulness, light-heartedness, someone who didn't take life too seriously. I knew how he should look. I knew his body type. I knew his political leanings. I knew he had to love cats. But I had to be open-minded about this. I knew the more conditions I put on my manifestation, the less likely it would be to come to me.

I found my mind going back to The Beautiful Mike and the lost opportunity. I wondered how it was possible to have that level of attraction between two people and have it go nowhere. Something felt unfinished. I daydreamed about him often and wondered if I'd ever see him again. With a sudden pull of worry that I'd be single forever, that I'd never find a decent man, I relaxed deeply into *trust*. And in doing so, I felt something similar to that burst of motivation that one has at the end of a disastrous relationship — a flush of assertiveness and a sense of possibility and hope.

It dawned on me that I needed to take action if I weren't to be single for the rest of my life. I needed to take a step in the direction of meeting someone. But I also needed to be completely open to things not turning out according to plan. I'd heard good things about an online dating site called Guardian Soulmates. It struck me that online dating would allow me to enjoy the process of finding someone without being attached to the outcome of any particular date. And even if I didn't meet the love of my life, I might make some new friends. I could treat it as a big game.

Literally within minutes of falling into trust, I had made a profile and uploaded a photo. That's all it took. Simply that one move in the right direction. I entered my details, and the algorithm sent me my matches. And top of the list, with a compatibility rating of 98%, was a profile with the nickname MikeyW.

I knew the face looking out at me. It was him. It was The Beautiful Mike.

Before my mind had a chance to kick in, think and worry and make up a reason to stop me, I fired off a private message. (My free membership didn't allow me to contact members, so it cost me £14.95 to send that email!)

I still remember the message I sent:

So, I was looking through Guardian Soulmates when I saw a face I recognised. Remember me? The barmaid from the Nag's Head? How bizarre is this? Get in touch if you want to meet up.

He replied almost immediately, telling me he'd love to meet.

The timing was exquisite: I couldn't go on a date immediately because I had planned a weeklong detoxing fast. I had already bought the equipment and didn't want to sabotage it. During that week, I had the most profoundly perfect detox. I came out with a clear head, perfect skin, a healthy glow and...almost inconceivably... I lost ten pounds. *TEN POUNDS!*

I went off to my date with Mike looking and feeling better than I had done in years.

The rest is history. We have now been together for more than six years. In that time, we have barely said a cross word to each other. We've had some disagreements, but we have never had a row or a fight, never shouted, never lost our tempers with each other. We don't hide things from each other. We talk about everything. He supports and inspires me, and I do the same for him. He is my best friend, and I am his. We have both grown immeasurably as people since we got together. And after all these years together, I still find him as beautiful as I did the first time I saw him.

My German boyfriend often rebuked me for being too eccentric, too silly, a 'nonsense person' as he liked to call me (and not in an affectionate way). After the misery of being with a man who valued seriousness above all else, I realised I needed *silliness* in my life. Mike has buckets of silliness. Mike and I often engage in nonsense talk, make up our own alternative words for things, and have a sort of ridiculous comedy sub-text running alongside our everyday lives.

Some people love books or films or football. Mike loves comedy, often watching hours and hours and *hours* of it. But he not only loves comedy, he *studies* comedy, appreciating it as an art form. He's interested in the devices comedians use, the structure of effective jokes, its history, its place in different cultures. If Mike had ever decided to complete a PhD, it would have been in comedy.

I asked for a man with a good sense of humour — and the universe gave me a man whose very *passion* is humour.

Is it any wonder I believe in magic?

15. The Taming of Money

The inspiration for manifesting money came from an entirely unexpected place.

I must have read pretty much every self-help book on the market in an attempt to beat my insomnia, but it was the wisdom contained in a book called *The Effortless Sleep Method* that seemed to do the trick. The author, Sasha Stephens, encouraged the insomniac to take responsibility for her own issue, to accept that she did not have a disease or clearly defined condition that doctors or sleep aids could 'cure' with drugs. Overcoming insomnia, she claimed, was entirely within my control. I loved this idea, and once I fully accepted it, I rapidly kicked my sleep problem to the kerb and began sleeping normally. After 15 long years of suffering I had finally managed to overcome my chronic insomnia.

As it turned out, that book would do far more than just help me sleep better.

According to Sasha Stephens, most people miss a night or two of sleep during a time of stress or irregular sleeping hours. But it only turns to chronic insomnia when we do some, or all, of the following:

1. Complain about how poorly we sleep;

2. Believe we are bad at sleeping;

3. Believe there is something broken or wrong with us;

4. Take sleeping pills (in other words, give up responsibility);

5. Jump on every last little thing that doesn't go right and analyse the hell out of it — the 'what went wrong last night' mistake;

6. Look to doctors or experts to put it right (give up responsibility).

In her second book, Sasha suggested creating a whole new identity for yourself — as an ex-insomniac, as a good sleeper. She advised speaking, thinking and acting from the point of view of a good sleeper, of living life from this new place. She often asked the question: *What would a good sleeper do? Do that.* She also liked to say *The Story You Tell About Your Sleep Will Come True.* As you might imagine, this idea of creating a new identity for yourself by telling a new story struck a chord with me.

Sometime in the past, from British author Paul McKenna, I heard the term 'poverty consciousness'. His approach, largely based on NLP (neuro-linguistic programming), involved 'reprogramming' your mind to replace this poverty consciousness.

The idea of poverty consciousness had been rattling around in my brain ever since because it accurately summed up how I had come to view my life. Despite the progress I had made in other areas, I still saw myself as one of the poor ones, as one of those for whom money was difficult or impossible to find. More recently, I also had formed the belief that I could manifest everything but money, that I was perhaps someone who never would have money, someone who perhaps never *could* have money. This was *my* story, and I told it constantly.

So you see, my very *identity* was that of a poverty-stricken person.

I noticed there was a similarity here. Sasha Stephens talked about creating a new identity as a good sleeper, telling a new story about sleep. Paul McKenna was saying something similar with his approach to money.

Could I decide to see poverty as equivalent to insomnia and sleep as equivalent to money?

In other words, could I tell a story of riches and become rich?

After all, I didn't 'have' poverty, just as I never 'had' insomnia (in the sense of a clearly defined disease). Insomnia was just a name I once gave to a condition I assumed I suffered from, and poverty was just a name, an arbitrary label I gave to a state I assumed I suffered from. Because, let's face it, compared to much of the world, or those who lived 100 years ago, I lived an abundant life.

But there was a further similarity between poverty and insomnia — both had come about as a result of what I did, thought, and believed.

Yes, yes, I *know* this isn't what I'm supposed to say. I know I'm supposed to say poverty is caused by all sorts of socioeconomic factors. People are poor because they are underprivileged, or undereducated, or exploited, or forgotten, or stuck. But that point had already been made a million times over, and blaming the government or rich people for my misfortune wasn't going to make one jot of difference to my bank balance.

Besides, I'm telling a story of how I overcame poverty. And *I* overcame poverty, not by campaigning for social justice, but by changing what *I* did, didn't do, thought, said and believed.

So how did I do it?

In learning to sleep better, Sasha Stephens warned off engaging in 'insomnia-reinforcing behaviours' such as spending too long in bed, napping in the day, taking pills, and complaining about sleep. But what were my equivalent *poverty*-reinforcing behaviours? It wasn't hard to see.

What I was *doing*:

I obsessed night and day about paying off my credit cards.
I was letting my carpet-less floor and ugly walls get me down every time I looked at them.
I talked incessantly about my money problems, the bank and the credit card companies.
I was still working for minimum wage, being treated badly, doing a tedious job in a factory.

I was buying all my clothes in Primark, and on the rare occasions I ate out, I would always order the cheapest thing on the menu, whether or not I liked the food (it was usually fish and chips).

What I was *believing*:

There's something wrong/different about me.
I'm not a 'real' person.
More misfortune is around the corner.
Good luck is usually immediately followed by bad.
I can manifest everything but money.

What I was *saying*:

'I can't afford it.' *All day every day!*

When it came to overcoming insomnia, the simple act of banishing the statements 'I'm an insomniac' and 'I can't sleep' from my vocabulary had had a huge effect on my ability to sleep well. I could now see that saying, 'I can't afford it' was the exact equivalent of saying, 'I can't sleep.' And so by repeating, 'I can't afford it' several times a day, I was keeping that money problem firmly in my life, just as I had done so with sleep.

I was telling the story that *I can manifest anything but money, that there must be blocks from my past that prevented me manifesting money, that because of my upbringing, manifesting money was harder for me, that magic didn't seem to work with money.* This is what I was thinking, and I was believing those thoughts. This was the thinking that looked true to me. And so it had become my reality.

This negative money talk had to stop.

To get over insomnia, I instituted a specific programme, *The Effortless Sleep Method*, with steps to follow and things to do. So, where was my programme for getting over poverty? In my journals, I'd made some notes about something called 'money managing' I'd learned from people like T Harv Eker and Elizabeth Warren. It seemed like a sensible idea, although it hadn't particularly resonated with me at the time. But with my fresh new eyes, money managing started to look rather like the equivalent of following a sleep hygiene program. In itself, it probably wasn't going to cure my money problems, but when combined with everything else I was doing to change my psychology, beliefs, and thinking around the issue, it might have a dramatic and massive effect.

Simply stated, money managing refers to the process of separating your money for different purposes, *before* you begin spending it, and a lot more emphasis is put on saving than on spending. If you currently have money problems, I can give you no better advice than to start managing your money. For more details read *Secrets of the Millionaire Mind* by T Harv Eker, *All Your Worth* by Elizabeth Warren, or the book I wrote on this very subject, *Becoming Rich*.

One of the biggest shifts occurred when I decided to manifest money with the specific intention of giving it away to someone or something I cared about. But this was not about vague monthly donations to huge multinational charities with directors on enormous salaries, or virtue signalling on Facebook. This was me helping the specific people and animals and causes that I cared about, and most of the people who knew me had no idea I was doing it. Some of those I gave to weren't even registered charities — they were just people in trouble. I began giving money to family members, to crowdfunders, to a harassed waitress, or a friendly taxi driver.

I'm not going to pretend this was utterly selfless. Far from it. This was still all about me. You see, when I gave money to someone who needed it, this act alone reversed all the negativity and feelings of injustice I had about myself. I could change a life I cared about simply by giving. I had turned from bitter, needy victim to financial saviour. I could be a hero every day through the simple act of giving to others. And how do you think this made me feel? Grateful? Empowered?

It made me feel bloody magic, I can tell you!

And the *really* weird thing was whenever I gave money, it would come back to me, often within 24 hours. I'd donate money and get a council tax rebate the next day. Or I'd be awarded an Amazon All-Star Bonus. Once, I kid you not, one of my credit card companies sent *me* a cheque, because they had apparently overcharged me some years previously. In each case, the amount of money I received was close to or *exactly the same* as the amount I donated. It was almost spooky.

I was money managing. I was refusing to complain. I was telling a new story of riches. I was giving money away and watching it flow back to me. I was a far cry from the miserable heap collapsed on a cold, uncarpeted floor.

The effects of these things combined were spectacular. Little by little, money started to flow in. First, it was the Russian translation contract I talk about in *Becoming Rich*. Next, it was four books in a hugely lucrative ghost-writing gig. I wrote a throwaway diet motivation book that often sold 20 to 30 copies a day without any marketing. That's more passive income from one little book than I used to earn working 12 hard hours in the factory.

Of course, I wasn't *purely* manifesting stuff out of thin air. I wasn't, as Mike Dooley says, 'sitting around waiting for Oprah to call'. I wasn't lazy with my magic. This was not, not *ever* about thinking nice thoughts of things you want and watching as those things fall into your lap. That's bullshit. Excuse my language, but I need to make that clear for the sake of those who still write to me every day to ask why their lottery numbers haven't come up yet.

The truth is, I was *doing* tons of stuff too. And I'm not talking about the sort of ordinary hard work I had done working long shifts in the factory. I'm talking about taking action *in the direction of my goal*. I was writing, I was building websites, I was sending emails, I was researching and reading and taking action every single day.

But now, with the addition of *magic,* everything became somehow charmed, effortless. Success became ridiculously, unfairly easy.

When I set out to manifest money using my new understanding, £36,000 per year seemed to me all the money I would ever need. It's incredible how small my goal was at first. But those tiny ambitions were easily achievable, and so provided a firm foundation on which to build a great magical empire.

If you'd like details of my fully-formed money creation plan, please do read *Becoming Rich.* Despite all my subsequent changes in understanding, this is exactly the same plan I still follow to this very day.

16. My Life Was Now Transformed

Life as a whole rapidly turned in my favour. I made a couple of great new friends, Sam and Dave, two people I felt immediately comfortable with. When another friend, Bertie, suggested the five of us go away to spend a weekend at his parents' cottage on the wild Suffolk coast, I jumped at the chance. That weekend turned out to be one of those magical times when you laugh like you've never laughed, when you tell ghost stories and rude jokes, and confide in each other. We bonded so tight on that weekend I knew we would be friends for life. To this day, the five of us (actually now six of us, now that Sam and Dave have a child) still visit the Suffolk coast twice a year.

I joined a local samba band, a source of fantastic community. I began singing in two local choirs, and I met two new great friends, Nick and Nicole, a local couple whose very existence is founded on fun. Socially, life had exploded.

My whole demeanour had changed beyond recognition. Gone was the sulky, dejected clod, drinking wine alone in front of the television. I was walking around in a state of gratitude, rarely really complaining about anything.

I was doing stuff, taking risks, trying things out. But I was so unattached to the outcome of whatever I was doing that I was able to contemplate the non-manifestation of my plans without fear or worry. I was able to expect the worst and be totally okay with it. Nothing was ever deemed bad or disastrous. I saw everything that happened as either good, great, or as a stepping stone to something even more fabulous. There was no misfortune, there were no disasters. I was 'letting everything be okay', no matter what. I *trusted* that everything, everything was working out perfectly.

When I tried hard to work out what was really going on, to think or rationalise my way to the truth, things would begin to slow down, become stuck, and I'd get frustrated. When I was able to trust, to let go of trying to work it out, things would begin to flow again. So I gave up trying to understand what was really going on. I let go and relaxed into not-knowing.

And precisely *because* I didn't know what was going on, it seemed to me the ideal word for *all* of this, was *magic*. I fell back on the ultimate 'cop-out' explanation — *it's magic*. But this was no coward's way out. Trusting in magic held great power. Magic was the sensation I had when I let go, the concept that *allowed* me to let go, as well as the force behind the mysterious way in which I seemed able to make things happen. Magic was at the heart of everything.

A Note About Snap-Backs

Before I go on, I want to say something. There is one part of my earlier writing I wish I could remove or recant. It is what I had to say about snap-backs. So many readers have latched on to the idea of this phenomenon and are now using it to characterise their whole lives, telling a new story of woe. People often write to tell me of the snap-backs they have been having, listing every unwanted event as an incidence of this phenomenon.

Let me make this clear: a snap-back is *not* simply a misfortune. It is *not* 'things going wrong again'. It is *not* magic 'not working'. It is not the ordinary misfortune of something merely turning out differently to the way that was wanted.

A snap-back is a perfect manifestation followed rapidly by the loss or cancelling of that manifestation.

But the way to deal with both snap-backs and ordinary misfortune is the same. Refuse to acknowledge any event as bad, as disastrous, or as a snap-back. In fact, obliterate the words snap-back, disaster, misfortune, and failure from your vocabulary! If you can learn to refuse to see any event as truly bad, you'll become more successful than you can believe.

In *Becoming Magic*, I talked of things turning bad if you don't get the preparations right.

I was wrong.

Now I realise there is no such thing. Things cannot go disastrously wrong, not ever.

For example, remember when I told you about the time I took an Aston for a test drive and how it left me humiliated? Well, it was that shameful event that led me to the 'magic of thinking small', something so incredibly valuable that I now make it part of my 'manifesto'.

Remember how much I deemed moving to London a huge mistake? Well, without London I wouldn't have met Mike.

Remember that poverty led me to depression and despair? Well, without that poverty I might never have discovered magic.

I could list dozens of events like this, and if you think about it, you can too. Look back at your life. Notice the way that events follow events. Some are good, some bad, some indifferent. Which actions led to which outcomes? Can you always tell? You can't, can you? It's impossible to see the end result of any particular action, event, or situation because the chain of events never stops. We never can see the final outcome of any given action, event, or situation because such a thing doesn't exist.

For a long time, I stressed about the fact that I could only see the value in an experience after the fact. Why couldn't I see the good in a 'bad' situation *at the time*. It seemed so unfair.

And then it dawned on me.

They are *all* good things. There *are* no bad experiences. There are only good experiences and stepping stones to something greater. Something you weren't thrilled with may have happened today, but something great might happen tomorrow as a direct result. This means you can choose to see almost any event as leading to something good. Things don't go 'wrong'. Things always, always turn out for the best. The odds are stacked in your favour. You're playing with the house's money.

So don't ask me what to do about snap-backs. Because there is no such thing.

17. Who Am I?
The Magic of Becoming Genevieve

This is a tale of two women.

Once upon a time, there was an author called Genevieve Davis. She overcame debt, poverty, overweight, loneliness, and a miserable life using manifesting and magic. She wrote four very successful books on creating a great life using 'magic', as she called it. Genevieve believed in magic, other forces, higher powers and intuition. She was spiritual, cosmic, and chaotic in her thinking. She hid her identity from the world, not even revealing her writing to her own mother and best friend. She never did interviews or wrote articles. She shunned publicity and largely left her books to their own devices, doing the bare minimum of marketing to keep them selling. Her books were uplifting, motivating but direct, straightforward, and no-nonsense.

Another woman called Sasha Stephens had a terrible problem with insomnia. After 15 years of suffering, she ultimately turned her life around, overcoming her problem using common sense, practical advice, and lots of experimentation. Sasha was science oriented, an academic, an intellectual, an atheist. She went on to write some very successful books on sleep and overcoming insomnia, including *The Effortless Sleep Method*. She became very well-known in certain circles, carrying out dozens of interviews and writing many articles on sleep. Her books and products sold all over the world, and her writing was translated into many languages. Her books were uplifting, motivating, but direct, straightforward, and no-nonsense.

Sasha suggested you take practical steps to reinvent yourself as a good sleeper.

Genevieve suggested you change *you* and watch as the world magically transforms around you.

Both approaches worked.

The two sets of books had entirely different audiences. They were read by different types of people, interested in different things. Essentially, they were both saying the same thing but using entirely different frameworks to do it.

Genevieve's books were spiritual, New Agey, inspirational, esoteric; whereas Sasha's books were entirely practical. Both looked at overcoming adversity and creating change in one's life but using entirely different ways. One was logical, scientific; the other was away with the fairies.

Have you worked it out? I'm sure you have.

I *am* Sasha.

Genevieve and Sasha are the same person. You see, I wasn't entirely honest when telling my history with Sasha's book. I didn't discover the book. I wrote the book. Everything else is true.

Let me introduce myself properly. My real name is Sasha Stephens. You already know I'm the author of four books on magic. And I've told you how 15 years of my life were almost entirely dominated by a severe insomnia problem. After exhausting all the options the medical profession had to offer, I eventually overcame the problem myself by changing the way I thought about sleep. Having beaten insomnia entirely, I wrote my very first book, *The Effortless Sleep Method*.

But I began to see that I could apply those principles to other activities. So I took my understanding of curing insomnia, and I added magic. In doing so, I made all sorts of fabulous things happen, including selling hundreds of thousands of books in multiple genres, both fiction and non-fiction, running four different websites, a sleep consultation service, an online insomnia recovery program and several diverse businesses. I attracted a large group of friends and lost weight. I also met a perfect man, in the most serendipitous way, with whom to share it. When an organisation I cared about became a victim of fraud and got into financial trouble, I decided to write a book to raise money for them. That first magic book was called *Becoming Magic*.

A lot of people over the years have asked me how I changed my life. I always fobbed them off with glib answers. And I would even put myself down. *I just got lucky. I've worked out how to game the system. It's easy once you know how Amazon works.*

What I never had was an explanation for the rest of it. How did I become so lucky in other ways? Forget the money for a minute, because it's always easy to give a more everyday explanation for that. What about the spookily perfect partner? What about the adventures I get to go on? What about all the varied and interesting things I get to do? What about the way things always seem to go right for me?

I never really gave anyone an honest explanation for this. I kept it quiet.

Well now, to those who know me and have wondered over the years, I will give you the answer.

I used *magic*.

I used magic to manifest almost everything I had ever wanted. Money, a successful career, a lovely home, no debts, a big, vibrant social life, and a sickeningly harmonious relationship.

But despite my belief in magic, I'm really not one of those cosmic, flowery types. I don't know how to feel my chakras or attune myself to energies. I don't consider myself 'a little bit psychic'. I don't think I was a high priestess in a previous life. I can't heal people. But I do have a mind that won't stop turning, like many of you.

As a child, I wanted to be a scientist, specifically a nuclear physicist, because I loved having my mind stretched in weird and wonderful directions. When my lack of mathematical ability put paid to that career, I turned my attention to philosophy. Philosophy taught me how to think in every which way, and then back again. It also drove me nuts.

Philosophy teaches you how to think, and how to argue, and how to construct a perfectly logical and watertight argument. But it doesn't tell you how to feel, intuit, or believe. If anything, it is positively hostile to such things. Philosophy also ties you up in knots and screws with your head. You can end up locked inside your own intellect, questioning everyone, never accepting anything, seeing a counterexample to everything, and never, ever really working anything out.

I've since learned that there are some things you *can't* work out. Sometimes you have to stop thinking and just feel. And sometimes, you have to let go of your intellect altogether and *trust*.

18. Sceptics and Dreamers

I never enjoyed my time in London. But a few good things did come out of my sojourn there. While in London, I lived in a flat with a fellow anthropology student, whom I have variously called Ella and Kerry in my earlier magic books. I'll carry on calling her Ella here, at her request.

Ella was an intellectual powerhouse. A visionary. She and I spent two bizarre, fascinating, wonderful, and terrible years together in London. Closer than friends, less conflicted than sisters, we lived effortlessly together like an old married couple. She was, and remains, one of the best and truest friends I have ever had. She had a razor-sharp intellect and conversations with her were as stimulating as they were amusing. We would often talk into the night about every matter under the sun. Ella was probably the most honest person I have ever met. While our spiritual approaches are very different, she was most certainly a major catalyst in my discovering what I call magic.

Ella had had a spontaneous enlightenment experience some years before I met her. At the time of her awakening, people around her believed she had gone mad.

Sometime after we moved out of London, I went on a walking holiday with Ella in Devon. By then, Ella had a grand plan for the future — to become a spiritual teacher, holding her own retreats — and she chose to view every event or occurrence as absolute proof that her wonderful plan was working out.

The funny thing was, Ella was running into all sorts of obstacles, but she didn't seem to notice them, never seeing the blindingly obvious ways in which her plan was *not* coming to fruition. She refused even to recognise the existence of any setback, of any news as 'bad'. How could such a sharp intellect pick and choose the evidence she saw? How could she be so selective with what she chose to believe? I started to wonder how much of her enlightenment experience had been real, and how much of it had indeed been some kind of breakdown. What I was seeing in her wasn't rational, it wasn't normal, it wasn't the way people are supposed to think.

Fast-forward a few years. Everything Ella said would happen had happened. Her whole plan had been realised. She now runs her own satsang sessions and retreats, both here in the UK and in India. So, honestly, who was I to judge her as insane? If she had listened to me, my sensible doubts, my reasonable concerns, my arguments for why she should question the apparent evidence she saw everywhere, then *none of this wonderful stuff would have happened to her.*

It was my experiences with Ella that gave me the idea for the evidence journal that I talk of at length in *Advanced*

Magic, a technique that became my favourite and most effective manifesting method. (It's also a big part of the way I overcame my insomnia, by looking for evidence, any evidence, that my sleep was improving.)

But there's more to be learned from my story. And it is this: don't listen to the sceptics any more than the believers. Sceptics are sometimes right, and dreamers are sometimes wrong, but scepticism has no monopoly on truth or good advice. If I'd listened to sceptics, I might never have left the factory. If Ella had listened to the sceptics who thought she was crazy (including me at one point), she wouldn't have had the wonderful life she has.

If I'm honest, I *do* care a teensy bit that in 'coming out', in making my true identity public, sceptics might be calling me insane, or misguided, or even a charlatan, that some of my friends may decide I'm not quite as bright as they imagined I was. But will any of that stop me doing magic? Hell no! Because despite the disapproval of others, despite all the intelligent scientific objections, *this stuff works for me.*

I also completely empathise with the sceptics, because there was always a big part of me that never really believed in magic. I met most of my friends while studying for my (second) PhD, at the University of Sussex, and many of these friends have doctorates. For a long time, I was what you might call a professional clever person. I did thinking for a living. And the circles I moved in were highly educated, scientific. *This* part of me was telling me this magic stuff was a load of weak-minded hogwash.

However, the *other* part of me, the less rational, more imaginative side was thinking something different. It was noticing that when I changed me, the world changed around me. I saw that something as simple as a change in attitude changed my whole day, not only in the way people reacted to me, but regarding the events, opportunities and luck that came my way. And I noticed that when I called it 'magic', instead of trying to explain it in some more scientific way, things seemed to work out even better.

Now, I'm perfectly aware that many of you may be reading this and thinking, *This woman is nuts. She sees magic. All I see is a bunch of stuff happening. Talk about confirmation bias! This isn't magic. It's just what happens when you change your attitude.*

Perhaps none of this is magic. Maybe there is no such thing as manifesting. Maybe there is a perfectly sound practical, scientific, physical or otherwise sensible explanation for the way I was able to make things happen, for the way in which I turned my life around. Perhaps my friends are right now talking behind my back about the way *they* think I did it. A change in attitude led to a change in action. Pure luck. Coincidence. Delusion.

But where's the fun in that?

I'm sure there exists a perfectly everyday explanation for what has happened in my life. But here's the funny thing: when I believe in a 'higher' or 'alternative' or 'unseen' power, *it works better*. So why would I ever choose to accept those other, 'rational' explanations over my own? Why choose an interpretation that doesn't work as well? That's not being irrational; it's *extremely* rational.

Call it something else if you like, I don't mind. When *I* call it magic, it works. When I trust entirely in science, it doesn't. That's not delusional, it's practical good sense.

I don't know exactly *why* it works, only that it does. And that, as I have said many times before, is precisely why I call it *magic*.

All this time I was working with magic, it was only Mike who knew what I was up to. He'd had his own spectacular turn around in fortunes. Since following my advice, he had gone from claiming housing benefit in a shared house, hiding away from the world, to running a booming photographic retouching business, working for the likes of Nike, John Lewis, and Zara Phillips. He was my one disciple.

But how could I tell everyone else what was going on behind the scenes? How could I tell my friends and family what I'd done to turn my life around? They would have thought I'd lost my mind. Worse, they might have ridiculed me, talked behind my back, pitied and patronised me. At that early stage, I was too fragile to invite those sorts of reactions.

I had already written books using other pen names in different genres. So I was very familiar with how the whole pen name thing worked. It was a simple matter to pick a new name and to write the magic books under an anonymous cloak.

Hence, Genevieve was born. I admit that this pen name initially came about because I didn't want to attract ridicule from my friends and family. But what started as a veil to hide behind became something altogether more powerful. Genevieve was more than a fake name. She became an alter ego, another persona into which I could step. As Genevieve, I was open to possibilities that didn't seem available to me as Sasha. I didn't have to be logical and smart and intellectual and scientific when I was Genevieve. I could be whatever I wanted. I was free to believe in magic, energies, spiritual stuff, chaos, irrationality. Heck, I would have believed in a flat Earth and unicorns if it had helped me feel magic.

If I had tried to science-ify what was going on, I'd have ended up creating theories, testable hypotheses, formulae, ten-step plans, and so forth. I'd have ended up forcing what I was seeing into a framework that wasn't suitable, a structure that would have killed off everything that made that phenomenon special. Calling it magic allowed me to stop trying to work it out. I was able to let it just be.

How did it work?

Don't know.

Why did it work?

Because it did.

I suppose this is my version of 'God works in mysterious ways'.

As time went on, I began to enjoy the anonymity for its own sake. The truth was, being Genevieve was also pretty exciting. Even my own mother and best friend didn't know I had written those books. So I went about my life with this big fat secret — a secret that made me feel powerful simply walking down the street. In many ways, this secrecy seemed to become part of what made the magic work, and I began to believe that by revealing my identity, I might somehow 'break the magic'.

I've kept Genevieve a secret for over three years.

What I didn't know at the time was that becoming Genevieve allowed me to connect with something huge, something fantastical, the source of all things. In *becoming Genevieve*, I was able to *become magic*.

When I became Genevieve, when I acted from a place of being her, when I tried to think as she would think and act as she would act, something amazing would generally happen. Genevieve was everything I wanted to be. She had a great life, lots of money, friends, a boyfriend. Genevieve didn't live in fear and poverty. Genevieve inspired people. She didn't let the everyday trials and tribulations of life get her down. Genevieve never read the news. She had no political opinions. She didn't submit to pressures to be a certain way, or act a certain way, or write a certain way.

Genevieve was the best of me.

So, what has changed? Why reveal myself now?

Well, all those years I had *decided* to believe in magic, I had *chosen* to describe things in my life as involving it. I would jump into the Genevieve identity when necessary because there I was free to believe what I liked. But now, following the events I am about to tell you about, I no longer have to suspect, decide or choose. Because now I *know*. Magic is real. End of story.

Anyone who tries to prove I'm talking nonsense because *science*… Well, they simply have it wrong.

They don't have a different opinion. They have it *wrong*.

Because of this, I no longer have to hide. I can be magic as Genevieve *and* as Sasha. The two identities can merge. I can become one. I am Genevieve, *and* I am Sasha.

So that's my story. That's the truth of my past and my identity. Probably not as exciting as you were hoping. I apologise to those of you who were convinced I was actually JK Rowling. It's incredible and hugely flattering how many of you thought this. But no, I'm not that famous. If you have ever endured chronic insomnia and read books to help, it's likely you'll have heard of me. If not, I'm going to be a total stranger to you. I'm an ordinary British woman. I live on the south coast of England with my partner, Mike, and my two Siamese cats. I'm now 49 years old and as ordinary as any of you.

I'm also perfect, fantastic, clever, talented and exceptional — *just like you!*

19. My Personal Prescription

Like a lot of people, I'm not a fan of following orders. I've never been good at bowing to authority. I find the idea of being ordered to do something I don't necessarily agree with by someone younger and less intelligent than me simply because they are paying me some money quite bewildering. This sounds like I'm being an awful smarty-pants about this, but the truth is, this attitude has its drawbacks: I've been sacked from or walked out of almost every job I've ever had.

It turns out this unwillingness to follow the words of another was really quite portentous. Because one of the absolute cornerstones of my philosophy of magic is that it is by looking to yourself — to what is true for you, not by being told, not by following orders or instructions — that you'll come to an experience of magic.

In coming up with my 'manifesto', I asked myself one question: *What is true for me?* And so it was that I formulated a set of guidelines, based not on the instructions of others, but on my own experiences and observations. There's a lot more detail in my four magic books. But they can be summarised here:

1. When I stopped all complaining and refused to say or think anything mean or nasty about anyone, life seemed to pick up, and nice things would happen.
2. When not complaining was combined with feeling *gratitude* on a regular basis, the result was even greater.
3. It is *essential* to combine this with *action*. When I tried to manifest, using law of attraction techniques and waiting for change, nothing ever happened.
4. There are no disasters, there are no 'things going wrong'. There are only stepping stones to something greater.
5. Small shifts lead to huge changes, aka 'the magic of thinking small'.
6. Thinking dispassionately about the very worst-case scenario and finding a way to be okay with it, results in things turning out for the best. This seemed to negate the whole 'thoughts become things' theory.
7. When I no longer wanted or needed, or had forgotten I'd even asked for a thing, it would suddenly appear in my life.
8. The most profound experiences in life had come when I became *magic*. I came to call this magic feeling *the receiving state*.
9. Magic is not something you *do*, magic is something you *are*.

These were not things I had read in someone else's books. They were not the standard dogma. They were what worked *for me.* They had come from my *actual* life experience of this stuff *actually* playing out. These were my (very loose) rules.

They are **not** *your* rules.

If there's one lesson I want you to take away with you from this book, it's that always, always, always your best teacher is *you.* This is what I'm trying to point to when I encourage you to take responsibility. I cannot teach you anything. I am just a signpost. I'm merely trying to head you in the right direction. Nothing more. I am not your guru. I am not even your teacher.

And I'm not saying this in a falsely modest way. I'm not saying it in a *don't follow me because I'm not really that special* kind of way that draws sharply into focus how special I *really* am. I'm not a teacher because *this is not, not, not about doing what I say.* If I tell you what to do, and you go away and do it purely because I said so, *nothing* will happen. If you want to learn something from me, you have to go away and *live* this.

It has to come from you. It is *you* that becomes magic.

It's *never* because you are doing what I say. It's when you are doing what you know or feel to be right. You can't be taught this stuff. You have to see it. You have to know it. You have to feel it.

In this book, I haven't given anything in the way of precise instructions for manifesting. This is partly because I want you to move away from any notion of following instructions and instead move toward looking to the truth of your own experience. But there's another reason — Having told you all about how I mastered magic and used it to manifest a perfect life,

I am now about to turn my back on almost all of it.

PART 3
THE DARKEST
HOUR IS RIGHT
BEFORE THE DAWN

20. Money Can't Buy Happiness (No, Really, It Can't)

Over time, I came to be able to manifest pretty much anything I wanted. My fiction and self-help books were selling incredibly well. It seemed all I had to do was write 30,000 inspired words on any subject and the book would sell. I managed to pay off every penny of my overdraft and my enormous credit card bills. After over 20 years of living in various levels of debt, I no longer owed a penny to anyone — something that gave me a huge feeling of pride and accomplishment.

I had even manifested a dream business opportunity. I had asked the universe for a business partner who could handle the marketing side of things (something I have never been good at). I would provide the content, and he would handle the rest.

Well, the universe had responded. An honest-to-God multimillionaire contacted me out of the blue on Facebook, of all places. Jake had sold his first business for $300,000,000. But it seemed even millionaires can have terrible insomnia. Jake had picked up a copy of my first book, *The Effortless Sleep Method*, and, having cured his problem, he now wanted to work with me. We were working on a project to create an online insomnia-busting program that would sum up all the best advice I had to give. I had moved completely away from writing books about sleep and no longer offered individual sleep consultations. So I decided to pour all of my very best sleep advice into one great product — an online program, based on the very best insomnia-beating advice I had to give. I worked damned hard to create a product I was proud of — my 'final hurrah' in sleep advice. Jake was a super-nice guy and easy to work with. This project could well take me from wealthy to absolutely stinking rich. The manifestation seemed perfect. The result of an intention put out to the universe *years* before.

Mike and I bought our first house together in one of my favourite parts of town, close to my mum, close to my son, close to my favourite coffee shops, and only a couple of minutes' walk from the sea. My home office was a big bright, gorgeous loft conversion, the best room in the house. I now had the house, the car, the man, the money, the friends, and my large passive income meant I could work as and when and *if* I wanted.

Of course, I was happy…

…wasn't I?

Well, for a while, this *did* seem to keep me happy. For several years, I basked in secretly 'being Genevieve'. I loved my new life. I felt like the luckiest person in the world, feeling joy every single day. I felt enormous fulfilment from having worked it out, from writing books that seemed genuinely to be helping people all around the world to experience the same kind of life I did. I had even attracted a tribe of devoted followers. Every day I would receive grateful messages from readers, telling me how inspirational they found my writing.

I was living an idyllic life. I got to sit in cafés, writing books, before going home to my lovely man and my lovely home and my lovely friends. I had no major pressures, no stresses, no boss telling me what to do, and not a penny of debt. I was educated. I was healthy. I was middle class. I had everything going for me. I was the luckiest person I knew. I kept telling myself this, over and over.

As time went on, the first flush of my magical success began to feel normal and everyday. I was still able to get pretty much whatever I wanted, materially speaking but cracks started appearing. Everything was sort of *flat*. I even found an occasional return of the old low moods that had afflicted most of my life.

But how could this be? My life was perfect. I was the golden girl who taught other people how to improve their lives with magic. How was it possible for me not to be enjoying mine? I had no *right* to be unhappy.

I took a good hard look at my life over the past few years. It seemed to me that manifesting all those things had proved to be an excellent distraction from the depression that had dogged my entire life. It even gave me a semblance of happiness for a long time. For several years, the thrill of having turned my whole life around was enough to keep me feeling good. I imagined I had manifested happiness, but all those years I had been living on borrowed time. Slowly, almost imperceptibly, that thrill began to wear off.

I'd planned exactly how my life would look and feel when I was rich. But that vision was way off the mark. Once upon a time I would look at smartly dressed women with envy and think about how amazing they must feel. It turned out I hated shopping, particularly for clothes. I came to see designer clothes as silly and ostentatious. I had already bought all the necessities, and now that the bigger, flashier things were there for the taking, I didn't want them. The poser car started to make me feel ridiculous. I felt like the worst kind of fashion victim, wearing that car like a badge of status. Some of my friends lived on benefits; how could I turn up to meet them in that car? It ended up being locked in its garage for longer and longer periods of time.

I ended up giving more and more away to charities, to crowdfunders, to waitresses, to *Big Issue* sellers, beggars, anyone, all in an attempt to find some satisfaction or happiness. I gave thousands to my son, Robin. I'd usually get a burst of good feeling when I gave to charity, paid for the round, or helped someone in trouble, so that's where most of my money ended up going. But this didn't make me a good person — I was doing it entirely for myself.

Then, the 'perfect manifestation' of Jake, the multimillionaire marketing guy, started turning a little sour. I had spent a whole year creating the new sleep product, and during this time I had to learn how to record and edit audio files, create a PowerPoint presentation, and master online course creation platforms. But the whole thing turned out to be something of a disappointment. The project wasn't working out. Despite pouring money into the site, the product was making no money.

How could this most perfect of manifestations not be working out?

I started throwing myself into work at any opportunity I could, all in an attempt to earn more money and create a bigger and better life. I wrote more and more fiction books, I took on more ghost-writing, I said yes to anything, as long as it allowed me to write. I'd sit there in my café with my laptop in front of me, coffee on my right, notebook on my left, and I'd feel all was well with the world.

At the time, I labelled myself a workaholic. It seemed I was using work as an escape in the same way that a drug addict uses drugs. Because whenever I stopped writing and went back to 'real life', the unhappy feelings would rear up again. Moods set in. The long bouts of depression were back.

Unless I was writing, I wasn't happy.

I threw myself back into a new crime fiction series (it was never finished, so don't ask for the title). I also had two new magic books on the go. One was about manifesting weight loss, the other was to be called *Ultimate Magic*.

Ultimate Magic was to be my best work yet — it was about the inconceivably effective combination of magic and action. It would show people how they could become truly exceptional human beings, by *becoming magic* and by taking concrete *action* at the same time. The perfect combination of spirituality and practicality, it was to be my *magnum opus.* But the book never was finished. My heart wasn't in it anymore.

I did seem able to manifest *things*. Things in the world. But once it had truly dawned on me that I was *not* able to manifest happiness, my interest in magic began to wane. My readers were clamouring for more, and I could so easily have churned out a few more manifesting books. But part of me was actively resisting. I knew, deep down, something was wrong.

Surely, if the circumstances of my life were right, I would be happy, wouldn't I?

I was coming to the conclusion that this simply wasn't true. I had spent my life chasing money, absolutely sure that my poverty was the only thing keeping me from happiness. But now, I'd paid off all my crippling debt. Not only that, I had the partner, the house, the car, the lovely family, the tons of friends, the rewarding career, several successful businesses, the money. So why did I often feel so profoundly miserable? The happiness I thought I had manifested with 'magic' was turning out to be nothing more than one long high.

Now the high was over, and I was dealing with the come-down.

I still believed what I was preaching, kind of, but my heart wasn't in it anymore. All of the integrity that earned me such an enthusiastic readership *was gone*. How could I carry on teaching more of the same? I could help people to bring pretty shiny things into their lives, but I also knew this would have no effect on their long-term wellbeing. Happiness wasn't *in* the outside world, not for me, anyway. I knew that absolutely. So how could I carry on writing books pushing people to improve their external circumstances?

It wasn't right.

It wasn't true.

And it sat *really* badly on my conscience. My readers believed me. They trusted me. I couldn't send them down that garden path any longer.

I came to realise that there is a rather sick and twisted benefit to having money problems — it does an excellent job of covering up all that is truly wrong in your life. It gives you a sense of purpose, a reason to get up in the morning, and it even provides you with hope — that *things will all be okay, if only I can get some more money.* Having money problems had given me hope for a better future.

Now, imagine the horror of realising that even this hope *was lost.* Because the future had arrived, and it wasn't any better than the past.

Then came the day my sister handed me a copy of *Eat, Pray, Love.* I read it voraciously. It struck such a chord with me. Here was a woman who, like me, appeared to want for nothing except happiness, the only thing in life worth having. When I read the reviews for *Eat, Pray, Love,* I was shocked to see so many bad ones. I also noticed that most of the negative comments ones were from people furious that a woman with so much, materially speaking, had the audacity to be unhappy. How *dare* she not be happy, when she had so much? Readers seemed genuinely angry at this apparently spoilt, overprivileged, educated American brat having the nerve and ungratefulness not be satisfied with her lot, to feel the need to go 'searching for herself' like some self-obsessed narcissist.

When I read the reviews, I wept. Because they all had it so *wrong*. And I could see that I too, had got it terribly, terribly wrong.

Like the author, Liz Gilbert, I had *everything*. I had manifested a charmed life, a 'privileged' life, an almost idyllic life. But none of it had made any difference, long term. I tried manifesting happiness. But it didn't work. The truth was, I wouldn't have known real happiness if it bit me on the bum. I knew elation. I knew the ego boost that came with success. I knew feeling pumped up. I knew the high of getting a sudden influx of cash, or a bestseller. But these things lasted weeks or days or hours.

As the months went by, one thought was slowly, creeping into my consciousness — *there's not one thing you can buy, not one thing you can own, not one circumstance you can manifest that will make you happy.* This idea began to torment me until eventually, it totally took me over.

It was pointless trying to change the outside world. This was an inside job. I needed an epiphany, some an aspect shift, after which nothing would be the same again.

I needed the big awakening.

21. *'Just Look Within'* — Yeah, right!

Because of my history of insomnia, I have tried a lot of different types of meditation over the years. I learned Transcendental Meditation, Buddhist meditation, and Zen, all in an attempt to sleep better. During that time, I heard tales of awakening experiences and spiritual enlightenment. I heard that reality is nothing more than an illusion, that beyond our little ego minds is a bigger expansive mind. I heard that this 'Big Mind' is infinite, is everything, that we are all one.

It all sounded rather fanciful, but these ideas weren't coming from crackpots. Many highly respected and intelligent people held such views, including my good friend, Ella — as I mentioned earlier, one of the keenest minds I have ever known.

Most of the gurus and the great masters had said something similar. 'Look within', they all said. 'Watch your thinking', 'Happiness is not outside you, it's inside you', 'What's behind the thinking?', 'Look for the source', 'Meditate, meditate, meditate!'

The truth was, I'd been meditating and practising self-inquiry for almost 15 years, and none of it had made a blind bit of difference. During the two years I lived in London with Ella, she and I would have long, inquiring conversations in which she'd guide me to *look within*, trying in vain to point me to what she could see so clearly.

'Where is the I?' she'd ask.

'Here,' I'd say.

'Who's saying that?'

'I am.'

'Where is the source of the "I am"?'

'I don't know! Look, this is giving me a headache.'

'Who is it that's having the headache?'

'Me.'

'Whose voice is that?'

'MINE!'

She would patiently continue asking those self-inquiry questions while I would cry with frustration. Ella also introduced me to Mooji, a twinkly, Father Christmassy teddy bear of a man. Mooji exuded peace, calm, and smiles, and I went to hear him speak in London several times. But listening to Mooji just brought up the same frustrations. It all sounded like a nice idea, but I never really had any clue what he was talking about.

My greatest desire, my number one 'intention' was to discover more about The Glimpses. Instinctively, I knew that all I sought was to be found within them. I knew they often came when my mind was in a quiet, open, gently contemplative state. I knew they felt fantastic, better than any earthly pleasure. But in all this time, I hadn't moved one step closer to understanding them or to summoning them at will. The Glimpses remained mysterious and elusive.

After years of going round in spiritual circles with Ella, Mooji, Eckhart Tolle, Big Mind, searching for The Glimpse and all the various meditation practices, I gave up. Awakening or enlightenment was not something you could *do*, I decided. You couldn't 'get there', you couldn't 'go looking' and find what you were looking for.

Just because one or two people might reach enlightenment through deliberate means, it didn't follow that most, or even many people could ever achieve it. This was the story I told myself. Accounts of Buddhist monks spending 20 or 30 years fruitlessly searching only seemed to lend weight to my theory. Spontaneous awakening did exist, I was sure of it, but it was always just that — *spontaneous*.

I even became angry with those gurus who, having had an inexplicable sudden enlightenment experience, would then attempt to guide the rest of us to that state using various techniques that never worked. I came to detest their smug patience and their ever-present patronising smiles. They all seemed to be saying, *If only you sweet little mortals could be enlightened like me, you poor, weak, ignorant, deluded humans. There, there. Have a pat on the head and bask in my brilliance.* That's how I viewed the so-called enlightened ones I came across.

So I made a conscious choice to turn my back on this sort of spirituality altogether. I decided life inside the matrix was preferable to this limbo place. What was the point in believing better was out there but being completely unable to see or experience it? A life striving for awakening or enlightenment was no better than one striving for the next pound (or dollar) as far as I could see. It was exhausting, it was frustrating, and it was terribly, terribly disappointing. I'd rather leave enlightenment, thanks.

No, my only hope was to make the best of what I knew, to make the best of what I had — life, with all its ups and downs, its pain and its difficulties. I'd manage my moods, write books, get richer, and fill my life with more and more distractions. And who knows, I might find a chink of happiness here and there.

It may not have been the best life available to *anyone*. But it was the best life available to *me*.

22. My Final Day on Earth

For five months or so at the beginning of 2017, I had been on a downward spiral. By May I was in a really, really bad way. Unable to find happiness in anything at all, I was spending two to three days a week in a painkiller-induced stupor. My excuse was that niggling back pain required me to take the drugs. But in reality, I took them because they helped me to shut out the bad feelings.

My plan to live a life as full and distracted as possible wasn't working. I had tried getting back into the magic books, trying to 'chase the dragon' of the good feelings that came about when I first wrote *Becoming Magic*. But this time it seemed utterly disingenuous. I had written those first four books from a place of integrity, and now I didn't believe my own hype anymore I couldn't find the motivation to carry on writing them.

Then at some point in the spring of 2017, the dam broke. The thought overpowered me that there was nothing, literally *nothing* I could buy, do, or have that would make me happy. And with that, I stopped trying to convince myself how perfect my life was.

My life *wasn't* perfect at all. It wasn't even good. I simply had quite a lot of stuff. And if a good life has absolutely, utterly *nothing to do with how much stuff you have,* then how could I be judged successful, privileged or lucky?

Of *course,* my life wasn't good *because I wasn't happy.* A million pounds? A million billion pounds would have made no difference because there was not one single thing I wanted to buy.

I fell into a deep, deep depression. The notion of taking my own life wasn't attractive, and I have never been suicidal. But I found myself looking forward to being an old lady so that I could die quietly, without causing a fuss.

I wrote a journal entry around this time that pretty much sums up how I felt. This is it, word for word. Please excuse the foul language. But remember, I was in despair and at the end of my rope.

I'm absolutely, completely f***ed off. I hate everything in my life. I'm bored. I'm anxious. I'm depressed. How can you be bored and anxious at the same time? Well, I am both right now. Nothing has any fun in it. Nothing contains any joy. The only time I'm happy is when I'm f***ing wasted on booze. Then a pretend euphoria will come over me and make me think I'm happy. Except six hours later I'll wake up with a pounding heart, racked with paranoia and regret. I have no escape from the depression right now. How did my life become this? How did I lose all joy and ability to have fun?

I literally do not know how to be happy anymore. I don't even really remember what that feels like.

One thing is for sure... nothing external will help with this. This indeed is 'all about me'. A lot of people would swap their lives with mine, I know that. But no one would trade the way this life feels. One minute in my head right now and the unemployed single mother homeless crack addict would run screaming back to her own life of poverty and deprivation.

You want to know why so many wealthy people are unhappy, despite all that money? It's not because they are spoilt or ungrateful. It's because they have come to that realisation that there isn't a single thing they can buy or pay for that will make them happy.

Part of me strongly suspects there is a deeper, more fundamental issue...

I really am one of the broken ones. Either born with faulty wiring or bad genes. I'm not special. I'm not unique. I am one of the most tedious group of people on earth. I'm just one of those self-obsessed, impossibly dull, permanently depressed people.

I am completely f***ed. Permanently. Incurable.

No one knew. No one knew what a terrible state I was in. I didn't share this with anyone, not even with my lovely partner, Mike. To the outside world, I was a picture of happiness, success and normality. I wrote books, saw friends, went to parties, attended events, ate, drank and exercised...

...and all the while I was screaming inside. I started sleeping longer and longer, usually getting ten or eleven hours of sleep per night. I'd get mysterious three-day viruses that would wipe me out and then miraculously disappear. When they started getting closer and closer together and lasting longer and longer each time, I began to wonder if I was coming down with chronic fatigue syndrome. I even began fantasising about being single again so I didn't have to keep up the pretence of normality in front of Mike.

I simply wanted to rest, and be miserable, and fade away quietly in a corner.

Decisions became impossible. But I'm not talking only about where to live, or what to do with my life. I meant things like, did I want to watch *Homeland* or *Downton Abbey?* Did I want coffee or tea? Coffee. No, tea! No... coffee? Every tiny decision became a dilemma. I was overwhelmed by worries about what people thought of me. I began to shun anyone in my social group who so much as looked at me funny, for fear they hated me. I felt wrong, crazy, messed up, and hopelessly broken.

I found myself longing for my days of poverty, the days when the ideas for new books would come to me and I'd get a flush of excitement. At least back then, I had a purpose. With big debts and bills to pay, I *had* to get up, go to work, and look for new ways to change my life. I had direction. Those were simpler days. They weren't great days. But they were better than this.

I touched on this issue in *Becoming Rich* when I talked about the days when I gave up work in the factory and played *Bioshock* for weeks on end. Back then, I had distracted myself with a new book project, with raising loads of money for charity, which made me feel I was making a real difference in the world.

Once again, I needed something to distract me from the aching misery that lay inside me. But I also knew that would only ever be a stopgap, a sticking plaster. That knowledge left me with no real motivation even to go looking for a new distraction. I knew I was heading for a breakdown.

I was slowly but surely giving up. I was giving up on life.

Friday, 12th May 2017, we celebrated my son's birthday. He and his girlfriend came with us to dinner at a lovely restaurant in the countryside. It was a good day, and the conversation was lively. Just lively enough to distract me from the turmoil inside. It has always been the case that the louder the world outside, the quieter I am inside. Sometimes, when the outside world was very loud, I would feel a semblance of happiness. This was one of those days.

Having got through the afternoon quite successfully, Robin and Lizzie left, and I plunged. I sank low, really low. I wanted nothing more than to curl up into black nothingness. I wanted to cut off my head and lock it in a lead-lined box, just to shut the thoughts up. Too miserable to be around anyone, I took myself to the spare room to sleep, unable to bear the company of Mike next to me in the bed.

The next day I awoke with the weirdest premonition. *It felt like it would be my last day on this planet.*

I didn't mean I was planning to end things. It was not a remotely suicidal thought. The feeling was more fundamental, more profound than that. It's almost impossible for me to put it into words, but it was as if some impossibly huge thing was about to happen, and that I might not be here after that day.

It was a lovely sunny Saturday, and we had long planned to attend a street party on the adjoining road. Mike and I live in a lively, friendly community, and it was events such as this that had led me to choose this area of town, even with its small gardens and close-built houses. It was the kind of community I had always craved, and when I imagined my ideal day, my perfect moment, it would be precisely this. I couldn't have created a more perfect day if I'd had a magic wand. A glorious spring day with my beloved son, my mother, good neighbours, and Mike.

And all I wanted was to go home and hide. The wretchedness of that day I can still remember, although I can no longer feel it. The heaviness of the mood weighed on me like there were stones tied to my head, to my arms and legs, but I dragged myself through the day, putting on an Oscar-worthy performance of normality. Inside, the voice was incessant: *I can't cope. Someone help me. I can't go on. Please, please, make it stop.*

I sat at a table outside the pub, ginger beer in hand and looked at the happy, smiling faces around me. Kids, babies, yummy mummies and hands-on dads. Glasses of Prosecco, pulled pork rolls and clotted cream scones. Friends.

Laughing. Dancing. Live music. This was what life was all about. It didn't get better than this. I was sitting in the middle of one of the most beautiful, sought-after towns in the country, on a sunny May day, with my gorgeous boyfriend, three generations of my family, live music playing, food and drink on tap, with no money worries, a lovely home around the corner, an easy, stress-free career, looks, health and intelligence.

And I was pitifully, *achingly* miserable.

I had turned my whole life around, manifested everything I had ever wanted, and I was no happier than when I had lived in the tiny flat with the stick-on floor.

And then I realised, if I couldn't be happy here, with all this going for me, with all these things in my life, then I couldn't be happy anywhere. And that realisation, knowing that nothing in the world would ever make me happy, was one of the bleakest and loneliest moments of my life.

The problem was not in the world. The problem was with *me*. I was broken. I was faulty. I was incurably messed up. I was irrevocably and permanently f**ked.

PART 4
FIRST DAY
OF MY NEW LIFE

23. Going to See Michael

The very next day I went to see a life coach called Michael Neill for a small group session. I was in no mood for it. I had booked it months before, and if it hadn't cost me so much money, I might well have cancelled the whole thing. But that Sunday morning, I found myself on a sofa in a comfy sitting room in Hampstead, London, with Michael Neill and six other people to talk about the nature of human experience.

When I'd first picked up Michael Neill's books, his words didn't particularly inspire me. A year later I found myself booking a three-day intensive teaching with him. What had changed?

Michael's words had begun to appeal to me. One reason was that his life seemed to reflect mine. He had endured bouts of depression from an early age that had no 'external' reason. He had a lovely wife, a great job, loads of money, but for much of his life, he remained miserable. Just like me.

Michael Neill was a coach and NLP practitioner until his life was transformed by an approach known as *The Three Principles*, first spoken of by someone called Sydney Banks. Sydney Banks was a Scottish welder who moved to Canada, and while there had a spontaneous enlightenment experience. Sydney Banks was my kind of guru. He wasn't mystical or pious, he didn't wear robes or ding bells, and he didn't insist that India was the only place a person could find spirituality. He was ordinary. He was from Scotland. He was perfect.

Michael Neill, having been profoundly inspired by the teachings of Sydney Banks, was now spreading the word about this incredible, life-transforming, world-changing approach. According to Syd (and Michael) we are sitting in the midst of complete mental health. Essentially, there is nothing whatsoever wrong with us. Complete and utter wellbeing is available to us at all times.

I'd heard authors like Hale Dwoskin, Wayne Dyer, Byron Katie, and countless others say something similar to this — that we are perfect, whole and complete, just as we are. Within us, we have the answers to all the questions we could ever want. We have a well of infinite good feeling within us. Yada, yada, yada. I'd heard it a million times, and it hadn't got me anywhere.

Michael Neill was now sitting in front of me, saying something similar — *You don't need to go anywhere or do anything. You don't need fixing. You already are all that you seek.*

Yeah, right. That may be true for some people, but I was different. Michael needed to know, I was *properly* broken. This would never work for me. I was too messed up.

'I'm the one in the room that *never* gets it. I'm different to normal people,' I told him. 'There's something about me, a blockage or something, or a subconscious belief that stops me getting stuff like this.'

But he didn't seem remotely concerned. 'You have only one problem in your life,' Michael said. 'You think too much.'

Well, *durr!* Talk about stating the bleeding obvious!

'Don't try to work it out,' he said. 'You can't understand this intellectually. Don't try to make it happen. Don't try and work it out. Don't do anything at all. Just listen.'

So I carried on listening to Michael speak, trying to work out what he meant by 'not working it out'. In fact, I tried 'not working it out' as hard as I could, but I couldn't work out how to do that! I was going round in circles, getting more and more frustrated, and as usual, nothing was happening. It sounded merely like nice words and contradictions. It wasn't becoming clearer to me. I wasn't 'starting to understand'. I was still the one in the room not getting it.

And all that time, I had no idea that I was so close.

It was on the afternoon of the second day that it happened. Michael had been talking for about an hour and, sadly, I cannot for the life of me remember what he was talking about. I only know that I had become slightly dull-minded from a big lunch, the soft sofa and the warm room. I was a little tired, and I had become almost drowsy. I was listening to Michael in an entirely mindless way, *as if I were listening to music.*

Think about that. Think about the way you listen to music.

I began to become aware of a soft, gentle buzz that had arisen within me. A little like the warm glow of alcohol, but my mind was clear. The energy in the room had shifted somehow, and I think Michael had noticed what had happened to me. Rather than carry on speaking, he sent us off on a walk around Hampstead and told each of us to walk alone.

As I walked, I felt awake, clear and good. I was gently elated, like I had been given some fantastic news. But my mind was calm. I wasn't going anywhere, so I walked slowly. It dawned on me how rarely we simply *walk*, without thinking of where we are going. How rarely had I spent a single moment of my life without considering where I was going, or what I should be doing, or what I would be doing *next?* And the amazing thing was, I was aware of this *without any conscious thought.* I had fallen into the present, into the now.

As I walked around the streets of Hampstead, everything looked fascinating. I wasn't thinking forward to getting back to Michael. I wasn't walking with any objective. I had no desire to rush, no need to get anywhere. I was happy just being alive. It was like a gentle bliss. I noticed three different species of tree I couldn't identify. They were so beautiful. I stood for a while and looked at their blossoms and at the curve of their trunks and the texture of their fantastic bark.

Back in the room with Michael and the others, everyone looked different. The previous day, I had gone into that room, looked around at the other people, and instantly formed positive or negative judgements about each of them. But now all those judgements fell away. Because now I could *see* them. Really *see* their humanity, almost into their souls. And it turned out they were *just like me*. In that instant, I knew for the first time what is really meant by the word 'compassion'.

I had discovered the part of me they were all talking about. I had found the perfect place. I had found the source of infinite wellbeing, in *me,* in the broken one.

The broken one wasn't broken.

I knew it like I knew the truth of my own existence. All that guff about true selves and unconditional love for your fellow humans and being whole, perfect and complete, and experiencing oneness with the entire damned universe…

It's all *true.*

Did you hear that? It's all TRUE.

From this new vantage point, everything, *everything* started to make sense. Suddenly, the spiritual messages and teachings *meant* something to me. I knew how to hear without trying to do anything. I knew what it meant to 'let my thoughts settle'. Even that most maddening of instructions, *don't try and work it out* made perfect sense.

From here I could 'see' my thoughts as separate from me. I could see that they had no power to hurt me. I could stand back and almost feel sorry for my thoughts, for how desperate and incessant and confused they were. They were trying really, really hard to make sense of everything, but most of the time they made it worse. I could see that no single thought was any truer than any other. They were all *just thoughts.* All the while they were fretting about, wondering and grasping, and agonisingly trying to make sense of things, I was sitting back and watching them, from my place of complete peace, wisdom and truth.

I was not my thoughts. Finally, it made sense.

I had been mystifying this whole business of awakening, of enlightenment for so many years, thinking there was a skill that others had and I didn't, or some special, mystery place, some direction I couldn't see. I even believed I might not *have* this 'innate wellbeing' thing, that I didn't *have* a true self. But once I 'saw' it, there was no trick, no special technique or mysterious direction to look. In fact, far from entering some otherwordly state, it was rather familiar and comfortable.

This perfect state, this innate wellbeing had been there all the time, waiting to bubble to the surface. Once I stopped interfering with judgements and trying so hard to understand, it had revealed itself automatically. All I had to do was allow my thoughts to settle, to quiet the ever-judging mental chatter, and allow the light to shine through. Perfection was part of me, built into the design of me as a human being

Yesterday I had been in a pit of black despair. Today I was perfect, whole, and complete.

The cynical amongst you might suspect I had gone from depression to a manic state. It crossed my mind too. But I could see very clearly that even the thought that *'I might be bipolar'* was just a thought, with no more truth than any other. Besides, this wasn't mania. This was peaceful, safe. It was warmer and fuzzier than the pumped-up omnipotence that I have heard characterises a manic episode. I felt more like a baby bird in a nest than Wonder Woman.

And here's the most amazing thing. I *knew* this feeling. I'd seen this before. I had experienced it many times, yet I couldn't say when or where. It was a bit like those times you recognise an actor on the television but can't remember from where. His face is *so* familiar, it's on the tip of your mind... but you just can't place him. What *was* this? Why was it *so* familiar to me?

When the three-day teaching drew to a close, I left London elated and content. I had certainly got my money's worth. But there was one thing bothering me. Michael had said, 'This isn't the law of attraction. This isn't like *The Secret.'* That worried me. Over the three days of the training, I had never let on to Michael Neill that I wrote books on manifesting and magic for fear he might somehow disapprove. Not wanting to spoil the experience of these new-found insights, I put the whole issue of magic and manifesting out of my mind for the time being.

But what on earth was going to happen once I got home to the reality of having written four books that might turn out to be completely wrong?

Seeing Caspar for the First Time

When I got back home, cool things began to happen.

I got awarded my first ever BookBub promotion on the first in a series of books that had stopped selling well.

I had longed to attend a particular event but couldn't because it clashed with something else. The day I got home, I discovered the date of the first event had been changed, and I was able to go to both.

My Korean publisher extended the distribution deal on one of my books for another five years, offering a new advance. *Free money.*

From perfect parking spaces to hotel upgrades, everything started to go my way.

I knew things were really different when I got a call from my mum. My nephew Caspar had refused to go to school that morning, and Mum wondered if perhaps I could get through to him. Could I have a chat with him, she asked. I wasn't keen. I usually tried to keep away from my sister's children. She has twin boys with ADHD, and by that, I don't mean they are simply rowdy kids who need to go and play in the mud and climb some trees. I once believed, like many people, that ADHD was a term that weak parents give to active children who don't get enough exercise. These boys had totally convinced me that, while I don't know what ADHD is or what causes it, it is completely real.

Caspar would sometimes act oddly in company, showing off, making stupid noises, silly faces, or staring at me to get a reaction. *Go away, Caspar,* I'd often say. *Stop acting like a freak. Stop being so weird. If you weren't so weird, people would like you more.*

I had said all those things. Some of them directly to him. He was 13.

But that morning, I walked into my sister's house and I 'saw' Caspar for the first time. By that, I mean I really *saw* him. I saw his pain. I saw his tormented little soul. And my heart almost burst with compassion for my troubled nephew. He was not a freak, he was not weird in any way. He was just a terribly disturbed and unhappy little boy. He was a little boy who needed help. A poor, sad, desperately troubled little boy. And I, his own auntie, his flesh and blood, had called him 'weird' *to his face*. His worst nightmare — that he was a freak and a weirdo, all coming true, reinforced by the people closest to him. How could I possibly have behaved in such a way? How did I ever think those things? All that time, all the years I had told him to shut up, to go away, to stop being weird...

I had been unable to see his *humanity*, blind to the suffering of my own family. Is it any wonder that people act the way they do to each other when I couldn't even see the humanity in my own *nephew*?

Once upon a time, I would become furious with people who claimed they had compassion for the whole of the human race. I was offended that Ella claimed to love every being indiscriminately. (Surely, I was more important to her than mere strangers?) But more than that, I flat-out didn't believe it. I considered it a bunch of huggy-kissy, virtue-signalling mush. Now, with eyes afresh, I knew what people meant by having compassion for criminals, even for the terrorists, warmongers and dictators.

My mind went back to my very first manifestation attempts. Years before, I had discovered that thinking good thoughts about people, *all* people, had a positive effect on me. But somehow over time, I had lost sight of that. True, I didn't complain outwardly as much, but I very often harboured bad thoughts toward politicians, public figures, terrorists, murderers, and big organisations. But I can honestly say, right then, in my sister's house, I genuinely had compassion for every human being in the world. Not for what they had done or the harmful actions they had taken, but for *them.*

Now, if you try to argue or convince someone that they *should* have compassion for terrorists and murderers, you will get nowhere. You will always collide with their previous experiences, their memories and beliefs about evil people and what we ought to do about them. But I hadn't come to have compassion for the whole human race after being presented with fresh evidence or a convincing argument. This wasn't an intellectual understanding at all. It was not something I had learned; it was something I could *see.* It was something I could *sense.*

I looked back to the bad relationships of my life — Stefan, the older German boyfriend and Rick, the abusive university boyfriend — and the bitter and angry political activists of the University of East London. And the animosity and resentment just *melted*.

I didn't actively forgive them. I didn't have to. There was nothing to forgive. *There never had been.*

Everyone everywhere is trying to be happy, and almost everyone is getting it wrong. And we are *all* doing the best we can *given our current thinking*. 'Everyone is doing the best they can' is not a bunch of hippy nonsense. It's true. It's really true. At that moment, I could *see* it.

But this first little epiphany was nothing compared to what was coming.

24. The Second Epiphany

Okay, that's all very nice, I hear you say. But what the blinking flip has this lovey-dovey stuff got to do with magic and manifestation?

It turns out, this has *everything* to do with magic and manifestation.

After I came back from London, there was one thing Michael Neill had said that still bothered me. He had said, 'This is not about manifesting. This is not the law of attraction. This is not like *The Secret*.' I knew other Three Principles people had said something similar. And so, I was left in a dilemma.

Michael Neill had opened my eyes to a basic truth, to *the* basic truth about my own experience of life. But what effect was this new knowledge going to have on my magical works? Were the things I had written about magic and manifesting wrong? Had I been hopelessly mistaken all this time? Was I going to have to recant everything I had said, pull my books from sale, apologise to readers?

Almost too afraid to face my old writing, I immediately threw myself into studying The Three Principles. For the next two weeks, I read everything. I downloaded audios, I attended the annual Three Principles conference in London. But something was stuck. Things weren't shifting. I just couldn't reconcile my understanding of The Three Principles with my experience of making things happen.

Then I realised... When I called it 'The Three Principles', studied The Three Principles, tried to understand things in terms of The Three Principles, I was placing artificial constraints around the truth. I was trying to fit everything into this framework, trying to force similarities between that and my own work, and desperately trying to explain my own previous experience in terms of Three Principles teachings.

It was Three Principles teachers who led me to this point. But it had to be *me* who continued on the journey alone. It's not that I had turned my back on the teachers who had inspired me, I just wanted to remain entirely open to all possibilities. By calling myself 'a Three Principles person', I felt constrained to stay true, to remain loyal to someone else's words. This constraint was stifling the truth. It was blocking my own wisdom. Of all people, I think Syd Banks (the man who first spoke in terms of these Three Principles) would have understood this.

So I took a dose of my own medicine. I put the Three Principles books down. I returned, once again, to the truth of my own experience, just as I had continually advised my readers to (and ironically, just as Syd Banks advised us to do). It was time to face the music, to own up to my magical past, to look at my previous writings and see how much of it was right and how much was wrong.

When I wrote those books, I did so with a pure heart and complete integrity. I wrote from my own experience, from what I deemed to be correct at the time, what I took absolutely to be true. So I really shouldn't beat myself up if I had got it wrong, I told myself. After all, people are allowed to change their minds. People's views are allowed to mature. People are allowed to make mistakes.

With this in mind, I went back to my own books. I went back to my own wisdom, back to my own writing, back to magic.

It was exactly two weeks from the date of my so-called 'last day on earth', that black moment when I realised nothing in the world could make me happy. I was sitting inside the same pub where I had experienced that dark, dark moment. I had with me a paperback copy of *Becoming Magic.* I opened the pages and began to read. My own words, published almost exactly three years before, and written even longer ago than that.

What a shock. What an incredible and fantastical surprise. It's true, there were some things I had written that sounded a little less convincing. But way stronger than that, there was a thick seam of truth running through all of my work. Not only was it not *wrong*, but large parts of my writing suddenly seemed truer and more important than when I had written them. It was the darnedest thing. Almost like I hadn't realised the truth of what I had been writing. Small, throwaway comments took on enormous significance, as if there were hidden messages in my writing that I hadn't even known were there. It was like the mystery subtext had now been revealed, and the truth was shining off of every page.

And Michael Neill was absolutely right that this understanding wasn't like *The Secret*. But then, why should that bother me when my work was nothing like *The Secret* either? My work was, well, it was *my* work. I had written four books explaining how I differed from many other writers. From the start, I had disagreed with the whole notion of a 'law of attraction', and I had never suggested you could magic things into existence by merely thinking about them. The law of attraction may have clashed with my new insights, but for the main part, my work *didn't*. My works weren't wrong. They were almost childlike in their naïveté, but they weren't wrong!

And that's when it happened...

The thunderbolt hit.

Everything clicked into place in the most significant, most powerful 'Aha!' I'd ever had. The gentle buzz came over me, and I fell into that place of perfect wellbeing, the place where I am not broken, and where *everything* makes sense. The stuckness fell away, and the magic revealed itself again. The truth shone through. Far from being incompatible with magic and manifesting, I could see that my recent discoveries weren't in conflict with magic. They were the key to all of it.

The perfect state of wellbeing that I had discovered — *I remembered where I'd felt this before.* It was just like suddenly remembering a film title, or a person's name — the name that's been on the tip of your tongue for days. I remembered where I'd experienced that place of exquisite perfection before.

It was the receiving state.

It was *my* receiving state. The one I'd been writing about for years. The one that had allowed me to turn everything around and bring wonderful things into my life. The one I was never able properly to describe, only to feel.

The most bizarre thing then happened.

The Glimpses started coming, thick and fast, dozens of them, one after the other. And then, actual memories began to pop up, remembrances of other times throughout my life when I had been in this same state. I remembered the day I left my husband and took the train to London and the shock allowed me to drop into a place of profound peace. I remembered walking on the South Downs, being at stone circles in Wessex, in the car on the way back from my one and only argument with Ella, and watching that final scene in *The Fellowship of the Ring*. These were times I'd had the strongest *Glimpses*. And as I witnessed these memories popping up, more memories appeared, and more, until they all sort of joined up together. Until I could see that the memories were no longer distinct — they all merged right up until the present into a feeling was here always. Underneath everything, in every second of my life was this exquisitely beautiful feeling — where everything made sense, and I was perfect and unbroken.

I had spent over 25 years looking for this. I had searched, I had yearned, I had meditated until I was blue in the face. And then, without trying, it *found me*. Here it was — The Glimpse. Communitas. The Receiving State. Divine Mind. Magic. *And it had been here all the time*. It had been sitting there all that time, under the thoughts, waiting for the chance to show itself.

I was whole. I was complete. I, like every other human being on this planet, was perfection itself.

From this new place, I could see the truth about magic and manifestation, really *see* it. Rather than undermining my work on magic, this new understanding only strengthened and added support to my early work. Some ideas that previously had merely been observations or hunches, now had a more solid foundation and an explanation. I could see this was going to change the entire way I talked about magic and manifestation. But at the same time, almost nothing had changed.

This second epiphany was almost more profound than the first, rocking my whole world, and putting me in such a state of power, grace, joy and optimism, the like of which I hadn't felt since childhood.

It's not like I was instantly enlightened. It's not like I was 'fixed'. And it's not that I didn't have tons still to learn. But *I knew life would never be the same from this point on*. I could start my life over again, at the age of nearly 50, and everything was going to be a big adventure. I had seen the truth. I had truly woken up. I was born again.

As I sat there in that pub, I picked up my journal and wrote an entry. I'd like to read it to you. Remember my talking about that black day at the local street party when I sensed it might be my last day on earth? Two weeks later to the day, I wrote this...

It is two weeks later. June 1st. I'm in the same pub, where two weeks ago I experienced my blackest moment. It is another perfect summer's day. I am sipping elderflower cordial on ice with sliced cucumber and mint. The doors are open and a breeze is floating through the pub, taking down the swelter of the day to a deliciously warm temperature. A song by Air— French Band is playing in the background.

I don't know if my life has ever been more perfect than at this moment. It is exquisite. I'd cry if I weren't so damned happy.

So what happened? Did I win the lottery? Of course not.

What a truly idyllic life I have now created for myself. A stunning life. Emotionally, spiritually, mentally, I have never been in such a good place, not ever.

My recent insights have led to a brand-new project. On this lovely day in the pub, as I reflect on the perfection that is my life, I have come up with an idea for a magical inner circle, where I will teach manifesting the right way, the true way. No more of the 'I don't know how it works, I just know that it works' stuff. Now I know the truth, and I know this clearer than I have ever known anything.

It is exploding into reality faster almost than I can keep up. It is tumbling, head over heels, tripping over itself, out of me, out of somewhere. Now I understand creation, perfectly. I understand manifestation. I understand magic. Those things I once just suspected were true are now open and obvious to me. I have manifested my wildest dream — the knowledge of how this manifestation thing really works. And it is now my human duty to teach it to others.

For the first time ever in my life, at this moment, I have no fear. Whether this project does or doesn't succeed, whether it comes into being or not, doesn't matter. I'm doing it simply for the joy of creating, for the genuine desire to make people happy. For the first time ever, the ride is more important than the result. And I know that because of this, it is all the more likely to work out, easily and successfully.

Perhaps the most amazing thing is that I have no idea how I'm going to do it! But no matter, because I KNOW that the universe will reliably dish the goods, and exceed my thought-based expectations every time.

I realise that from this place, I can pretty much create whatever I damn well please. I know that fear will no longer stop me. I know that I have the creative potential of the whole universe on my side. I know I can create anything I want. I know it's no longer about little me trying to make things happen in a big, bad, uncaring universe. It's not really about me at all.

So it turns out, this is all about manifestation. Except that now I can see how it really works, it doesn't seem so accurate to call it manifestation. It is creation. Creation by me, but tapped into the infinite power of the universe.

I have learned how to 'tap in', how to attach myself, and melt into the great potential, the great source of power, the source of all the good ideas and all the answers to all the questions I could ever wish to ask.

My job now, is to explain this to others, so that they can connect themselves up too. Except it's less like connecting up, and more like resting into, more like becoming it for ourselves. When we are aligned, when we are rested into that place, we will be able to create pretty much anything we damn well please.

All that time and effort I put into BECOMING magic, when all the time, I WAS magic

Those are the exact words I wrote two weeks after the blackest moment of my life.

For those who suspect I have described yet another a manic episode, you should know that in the ten months since that day, I've barely had a bad mood, let alone a depression. I might still have the odd low moment, but they don't last anymore. Now that I know how the mind works, I can't see how that would happen again. And ten months later, that plan I formed on the lovely day in the pub is coming to fruition. This book, my new website, and online course will be launched in the next couple of months. I haven't *manifested* them. I haven't *attracted* them. But with the help of the infinite wisdom and power of the universe, I have pretty effortlessly *created* them.

25. Creation, Not Manifestation

My entire life changed the day I realised my old friend, the magical 'receiving state' I had written about for so many years, was the source of the *Glimpses* that had fascinated me since childhood. Not only that, it was that same place, that same thing all the spiritual people speak of — what I often refer to as your 'inner magic' — the source, the Big Mind, the true, authentic self. Here was the receiving state looking me in the face again, but deeper, clearer, more powerful than ever before.

And that's when I could see it for what it really was.

It was not a *receiving* state at all.

It was a *creation* state.

A state of infinite potential.

All this time, I hadn't been receiving. I hadn't been manifesting. I hadn't been attracting.

I had been *creating*.

In the years after I wrote the magic books, thousands of people wrote to me. Many of them told me how my books had changed their lives, allowed them to manifest fantastic successes, life-changing events and people. But others reported no success at all. Some people wrote to tell me nothing had changed or that things had started going wrong again. I spent a lot of time trying to work out what separated the successful people from the unsuccessful ones. What were they doing differently? As the letters continued to flood in, one theme shone out the strongest.

Unsuccessful people hoped that following magical instructions would make something appear in their lives.

Successful people recognised themselves as active constituents in the process.

Unsuccessful people *waited for stuff to arrive.*

Successful people *made it happen.*

Unsuccessful people *asked.*

Successful people *created.*

I know this is starting to sound like a motivational sales meeting, so I'll try to explain it in a different way. More than ever, I could see that magic was not something I could pick up and put down. It was not something I could call on. The magical 'receiving state' offered a source of infinite potential. But *I* had to realise that potential. *I* had to bring it into being.

Some years before, I had made this same point in *Advanced Magic*.

The universe is very unlikely to offer you a lottery win, a surprise inheritance or a chest of treasure in the bottom of your garden. It is very likely to offer you opportunities… So do things…

It doesn't really matter what these first moves are as these will likely only be stepping-stones to greater things. Do anything as long as it is in the direction of something new or different. Keep your eyes open and when good opportunities are offered to you, take them. You never know where a particular move will take you. You don't have to find a million-pound business idea off the bat. What is important is that you are taking new steps, making new moves, opening new opportunities, meeting new people.

Don't wait for change, be the change.

But when I returned to these words after my awakening, I found they had taken on a new, more intense significance. I thought back to all the times people had told me about their plans to write books, set up companies, start new ventures, go to certain places. And then years later they would come and tell me the same story— they were still planning that same book, that same company, that same venture.

This had happened to me quite recently when a friend of mine, Roger, asked me for advice. He had a strong desire to get into virtual reality video games, something he was passionate about. But he didn't know where to start.

I told Roger that if I suddenly had an idea to start a virtual reality business, I wouldn't wait a second before doing something about it. I'd probably go straight home that night and make a list of first steps, things I could do or people I could contact. I might even fire off a few emails that very evening.

Roger was amazed. He had been overcomplicating the whole thing. So afraid to get it wrong, he had been crippled to the point of total inactivity. He had been thinking about this virtual reality business for two years, desperately trying to work out his first move. In the meantime, he told me, the industry had moved on by leaps and bounds.

It was then that I understood the source of the misunderstanding behind the so-called 'law of attraction'. I could see where I, and countless others, had gone wrong. Because there *was* a sense in which *thoughts* become *things*. But thinking about it is only the first stage. Thoughts only become things through a whole series of actions. Thought leads to action. Action leads to stuff happening in the world. That's how things change. But to take this truth and use it to formulate a 'law of attraction' whereby you can think up nice thoughts and then expect those thoughts to 'attract' physical objects into your life like a magnet attracting iron filings... well, as far as I can see, this is a gigantic misunderstanding of what 'thoughts become things' really means.

There really was a magical source of infinite power at my back. But it wasn't going to kick in if all I did was say a few nice affirmations and then sit like a sulky lump in front of the television and wait for things to fall into my lap. Yes, I could create things in this world. But I *couldn't* ask the universe to *give* me things. If I had done nothing but write a letter to the universe and sit back, waiting for results, nothing would have happened. I could ask for the means, the inspiration, the method by which I was going to create my desire, and *the universe would put these things in my path*. But the objects of my desire will (almost) never land in my lap without my taking action in their direction first.

After all, I can sit all day in a coffee shop, hooked up to that exquisite magical source of the good stuff, feeling love for the whole human race, and having fantastic ideas. But those thoughts and ideas are *useless* unless I open up my laptop and start tapping away. They are useless if I don't send the manuscript to my editor, commission a cover design, format the paperback, and hit 'publish'. It's all very well my sitting in a café with a gingerbread latte and having lovely thoughts. But that doesn't pay the bills. I also need to do a whole bunch of real-world things so that people read my books and I get payments from Amazon every month.

These are the actions by which *thoughts* become *things*.

26. The Strangest Secret of All

In the months that followed, life was like a beautiful dream. In The Glimpse I found everything I had ever wanted, all the good feelings, all the inspiration, all the belonging, all the connectedness, all the joy and love and friendship I had been searching for my entire life. All the feelings I assumed my desires were going to bring me. They were there for the taking. And *none* of them was in those things I thought I wanted so much.

The despairing moods seemed like a distant memory. The writer's block was gone. I excitedly set about writing the book you hold in your hands now, and it began flowing out of me like water. I have always had the deepest connection to magic while writing, and now, every morning I was there, in The Glimpse blissfully writing the book of my life.

At the age of 48, I was starting over again. I came to understand what people meant when they talked of being 'reborn'.

My *real* life had begun.

But I had been in a good place before. Might this be another instance of the 'post-self-help-seminar high' I had experienced in the past? I had heard many great speakers, been to retreats and trainings and come away uplifted. I had even done the famous weeklong Hoffman Process back in 2016, after which I had been in a good mood for months. Even after Hoffman, at some point the rot began to creep back in, the moods came back, and depression once again reared its horrible head.

But things were different this time, *qualitatively* different. I didn't simply feel 'good'. The change was far more fundamental — almost like my whole being had shifted. The effects of my awakening experience were not wearing off, *they were intensifying*, and my first 'epiphany' when meeting Michael Neill paled compared to what came after it. Every day that went by, life started to 'make sense' to a greater and greater degree.

Insights became so commonplace, I started to take them in my stride. And by 'insight', I don't mean I was simply having positive thoughts. Insights are not just nice ideas. Insights are something you *know*, at a deeper level. They are like truths you can suddenly see for the first time — truths that change your life from that point on.

About six weeks after my awakening, I had one of the most profound insights of my life. One that would have a colossal effect on my fears about depression and on my ability to create things. It was so huge, it could almost be viewed as an awakening by itself.

I was sitting, working in a Brighton coffee shop. A professional caregiver or nurse came in with two elderly people she was caring for. One old man and an elderly lady in a wheelchair. Shortly after they arrived, the old lady started coughing badly. She said she felt sick before vomiting violently onto the floor of the café. There was nothing particularly inspiring about this. It was the reactions of the onlookers that would reveal something truly profound.

Some people tutted and looked horrified, appalled, and a couple got up and left — for them, the event was disgusting, revolting.

Some people looked pitying and sorry for the old lady's embarrassment — for them, the event was sad.

Some children laughed — for them, the event was funny.

Some people pretended they hadn't noticed — for them, the event was best ignored and forgotten.

For me, the event had an entirely different effect. The manager of the café, a thin Italian woman of around 30, came straight out and, without saying a word, very quickly cleaned up the mess the old lady had made. The way she did it — quietly, efficiently, and without fuss — astounded me. She didn't have to do that. These coffee shop managers are not well paid. She could have insisted the nurse take responsibility for her charge. She might at least have raised her eyebrows or looked around at the other customers in horrified agreement. But she took it all in her stride.

That event had a strong effect on me. I was uplifted by it. I really saw something in that manager — a kindness, a decency, and a commitment to doing a good job even when put in a tough situation. I don't even remember what the old lady looked like. But I remember the manager. I still feel kindly toward her now whenever I see her working.

As I sat, considering the differing reactions of the onlookers, I reflected on something — What was the *truth* about that situation?

Was it disgusting, embarrassing, pitiful, funny, forgettable, or inspiring? They couldn't all be true.

And then it dawned on me. A massive, life-changing insight struck, after which nothing would ever be the same again…

When I had money, friends, a lovely home, and a stress-free job but was despairing — Was my life great or terrible? They couldn't both be true. The only thing that made me judge my outwardly perfect life as terrible was my *thinking* at that moment.

If we *did* directly experience the truth, the facts of the world, they would all be neutral. It is only thought that makes us have feelings and emotions, likes and dislikes and preferences, fears and joys. Without thought, we would experience the world as a rock does — completely without judgement or opinion.

I could see it. *Really* see it.

I looked back at the two blackest moments of my life. The first was when I was living in poverty and loneliness in the cruddy flat with the stick-on floor. The second was at a street party, surrounded by people I love, on a gorgeous May day.

The first time depression hit, it was easy to find a reason. My situation was not one that would conventionally ever be considered good. It was difficult, stressful, and lonely. I had little money, few friends, a rubbish car, and no boyfriend. I was working in a dreary dead-end job. It was obvious where to lay the blame for this depression. It had clearly been caused by my external circumstances.

But the *second* time, things weren't so straightforward. By any normal standards, my life was awesome. I had money, a partner, a lovely home and car, and an easy job. Yet I was miserable.

And it was here that the truth was revealed to me. If having money, a boyfriend, and all sorts of stuff *didn't have the power* to make me happy, then it follows that *the absence of those things never had the power to make me unhappy.*

I can't have been depressed because I didn't have a boyfriend. I can't have been depressed because I had no money. I can't have been depressed because I didn't have a decent car. *Not* having those things can't have been the cause of my depression because *having* those things didn't stop me getting depressed all over again.

Money can't make you happy, we've all heard that one before. Well I'm going one further here, it's not only money that can't make you happy: neither can friends, a boyfriend, or a lovely home. And when I say 'can't' I mean that *literally.*

This wasn't merely true for me, it was true for the whole human race.

It turned out there were some pretty big consequences of this insight. Because if there was no truth about a situation other than my thinking about it, then no one thought needed to be taken any more seriously than any other. So my thoughts *I'm broken and permanently messed up, I'm not capable of that, I'll always be poor, What if they laugh at me? There's something wrong with me because I should be happy in these circumstances* had no more importance, and were to be taken no more seriously, than *I fancy pizza for dinner* or *What lovely curtains.*

A gigantic *weight* was suddenly taken from my shoulders. Literally, I felt so light I could almost fly. I didn't have to worry about having to change the world anymore. I no longer had to worry about what people might think of me. I could stop fretting about getting my life just-so.

I had cured my lifelong depressions. *In an instant.* The crippling depressions would never return. This was no 'high'. This was *truth.*

I thought I had used magic to improve the circumstances of my life, to 'fix' those parts of the world that needed to be changed, to bring me people, money, friends, stuff. I assumed it was these things that had made me happy. When I fell into depression, I felt for some reason they no longer had the power to do that.

I fell into despair when I realised *there was not one thing in the world that could ever make me happy.* I imagined it meant something was terribly wrong with me. I believed I was broken or clinically depressed, that I was the one person who didn't find happiness in the world, that I had some flaw that made it impossible for me to enjoy life. But when I saw the truth, I discovered to my indescribable joy, that *this is how it is for everyone*. It wasn't a mistake. It wasn't something broken about me. It wasn't a character flaw. It was just a simple misunderstanding.

When I was happy, it wasn't because the money, the man, the achievement, or any state of affairs in the world had brought me happiness. It was my *thinking* at the time that felt good. When I felt bad, it wasn't because I *didn't* have money, a man, or any other thing missing from my life. It was only that my *thinking* had changed. I felt my *thinking* not the *lack* of money or a man or any other circumstance. Nothing in the world *could* make me happy, but there was no gloom and doom. Far from it. Because here's the fabulous flipside:

Nothing in the world could make me sad either!

I wasn't denying the existence of the outside world, but whether I experienced that world as happy, frightening, joyful, embarrassing, or unfair was only *ever* determined by my own thinking in that moment. And whether the content of my thoughts was positive or negative had nothing to do with what was going on outside of me. When my thinking changed, my experience of life changed. This, and only this, is how I ever changed the way I felt and *never* by changing anything about the outside world.

And here's the strangest thing about this. When I first *saw*, beyond any argument or rational understanding that this was true, 'Nothing in the world can make me happy' went from being the worst thought I've ever had to being the best thing in the world. The darkest hour truly is right before the dawn. Because my worst fear had revealed something magical, something spectacular.

If the world can't make me happy, the world can't make me sad.

If the world can't make me sad, there's no need for it to be a certain way.

If I don't think the world has to look a certain way, I don't mind what happens.

If I don't mind what happens, I can never be unhappy again.

And *this* is how I can claim I'll never suffer with depression again. My depressions, *all of them*, had been caused, not by poor circumstances, hormone imbalances, bipolar disorder, or any external reason, but by a simple but profound *misunderstanding*.

27. The Effect of All of This on My Creations

I sat there in the café and began laughing out loud. I realised that insight can come from anywhere, even from watching a woman vomit on the floor. For some reason, I found that immensely funny. People turned to look at me, mystified by my behaviour. First, an old lady throws up in the café, and now there's a woman laughing hysterically to herself. What a day they were having!

Boom! Laughter gave way to astonishment. I realised the consequences of this new world view. The effect that this was going to have on my manifestation attempts…. Oh my God, this was going to change *everything.* I was so excited, I could hardly type fast enough as the new thinking came tumbling out of me onto the page.

You may remember one of the fundamental teachings of my earlier writing is that continually asking and wanting *keeps your desires from coming to you.* Successful creation is about letting everything, every outcome, every circumstance be okay. The less attached you are to the outcome of your creation attempts, the deeper you enter the 'receiving state', and the more your wishes come true. At least that's how it seemed to me at the time. As it turned out, I was kind of half-right.

I always knew that 'letting everything be okay' had immense power. It was a large part of how I overcame my insomnia and forms part of my online sleep course. It also seemed hugely important to the whole process of making things happen. But I didn't really know how or why it worked, and it was always one of the most difficult aspects of the magical process to achieve at will. Ideally, I have always recommended having so little attachment to the outcome of your creation attempts that you don't care one way or the other whether you ever receive the object of your desire. I also know that for many people, achieving this state of apparent indifference was nigh on impossible. But now I knew that *nothing in the world had the power to make me unhappy*, I no longer needed the world to look a certain way or for things to turn out according to a particular plan. This meant that:

'Letting everything be okay' happens *automatically*.

Having attachment to the outcome *drops away*.

Grasping, wanting, and yearning for things *makes no sense*.

I got it. I saw it. I knew it was true with every fibre of my being. 'Letting everything be okay' and 'letting go of wants' was not, as I'd previously assumed, a *prescription* for entering the magical 'receiving state' — it was a *description* of what happened naturally and automatically when I did so.

Then I could see, *really* see, just how damned powerful I was.

Can you grasp the enormity of this? Can you get a sense of the effect this was going to have on my attempts to do magic?

Without the crippling prison of thinking I must change the outside world to be happy, I was free to create anything at all. All those hang-ups and judgements and fears that had stopped me pursuing my plans and dreams? Well… they no longer existed. Things couldn't 'go wrong' anymore because, if I wasn't attached to any particular outcome, they *couldn't* go wrong. I really could be, do, or have anything I wanted. The sheer magnitude of what was possible was starting to dawn on me.

I was going to be capable of *anything*.

In fact, you know that standard self-help question, *What would you do if you knew you couldn't fail?* Well, I had taken that little thought experiment and turned it into reality. Because, from this new point of view, *failure didn't exist*, it wasn't possible. 'Failure' literally made no sense.

You know, this is starting to sound remarkably like something I said at the end of *Advanced Magic*.

The signature state of Advanced Magic is the state of absolutely no doubt and no fear. It is when you feel so okay with the way your life and events are turning out, that nothing can faze you.

How good would it be to know that nothing would ever go wrong again, ever?

192

This really can be your reality.

See apparent disasters as stepping-stones, and nothing can ever go wrong again.

*'But, you're not talking about things **actually** turning out better; it's just you choosing to see them that way.'*

What constitutes 'turning out better' other than the way you see things? And what would be the point in things being an 'actual' way if you didn't see them that way too?

If you feel that things are going well, whose business is it to tell you otherwise?

If you think things are turning out perfectly, then they are turning out perfectly. And I mean this literally.

Advanced Magic is not about forcing yourself to carry on through adversity. It's about realising there is no such thing as adversity.

When this finally, genuinely hits you, you have no more worry, you have no more fear, and you are free.

And your life becomes one big game where nothing can shake you from your position of happiness and power.

Life really was my playground, where I could create stuff for the sheer hell of it, not because it was going to fix my life, but just because it's fun. I was free to do anything. Life suddenly became less difficult, less *serious*. I became light-hearted, brave, adventurous, fearless, magnificent. It wasn't just mishaps that were to be viewed as stepping stones. *It was stepping stones all the way.*

PART 5
AND THE UNIVERSE
RESPONDED

28. Something Frees Up

It was almost as if the recognition of this truth freed something up. I'd taken a step into a whole new realm of understanding, and the universe seemed to *notice*.

For some time, one 'failed manifestation' had been niggling away at me. I told you earlier about Jake, the multimillionaire investor who had contacted me over Facebook, asking to invest in my sleep products. When he'd first contacted me, I considered it to be one of the most perfect manifestations I had ever brought into being. But it hadn't turned out according to plan. After some time, trying to make it work, Jake made the decision he was out. He walked away from the project, taking his marketing advice with him. He handed the product, the site, the whole lot back to me to make of it what I could on my own.

I have always done my best to see apparent mishaps as stepping stones to something better, but I couldn't see the good in this. A whole year of work, for nothing. The universe had dished up the goods, and they were spoiled. There was no stepping stone here, this was failure.

Or so I thought.

Now, with these fresh eyes, I looked at the Jake situation again. It no longer made sense to view this as a failure when it had no power to make me feel anything. The only thing I had been feeling was my thinking about the situation. My thinking it was a failure meant that it *was* a failure. Now that thinking had changed, and the situation just didn't seem that *bad* anymore. And with that, it was as if something freed up. Something shifted.

Within a month, and without my spending a single penny in advertising, www.sleepforlife.com started to turn a profit. Not profit to the huge extent my millionaire investor, Jake, had wanted, but still a tidy income. Three months later, that site was bringing in more money than I had earned working full time in the factory — an entire living wage of completely passive income. This 'failed project' didn't look like such a failure anymore.

But that wasn't all.

It dawned on me that if it's stepping stones all the way, then perhaps *this wasn't the end of the manifestation.* After all, since the chain of events never stops, who knows where this might lead? The tension and regret surrounding the Jake project fell away, and I began to look forward to what might come about as a result of it.

I decided it was time to find a different person to help me with my future project. I needed to find someone who knew my books, who knew my business, who really understood me. Then a bizarre idea came to me. I would ask my readers. After all, who knew me better than those already familiar with my work? Almost immediately, I sent an email to my magic reader list. I told readers I'd had some recent changes in understanding and was busy working on ways to communicate them. I didn't mention that I wanted help. It didn't seem necessary.

I sat back and waited for results.

Within days, Melinda appeared.

Melinda Alexander Haseth, Founder of The Truly Group was one of many people who had responded, offering help. I heard from app developers, website designers and personal assistants, but something about Melinda immediately struck me. She had quite a track record, having collaborated with blue-chip corporate clients and some of the greatest spiritual minds on the planet. But more than that, Melinda seemed to 'get me', to understand my vision.

Melinda has become an indispensable sounding board for me. Her marketing company created my gorgeous new website and is helping me to create my new course. She was also a beta reader for this book, giving absolutely invaluable feedback on early drafts.

Only now can I see how vital it was that the whole Jake thing happened. Without Jake and the Sleep for Life project, I would never even have *considered* building an online course. I didn't even know these online course platforms existed. It would never have crossed my mind. Not in a million years. Without him, I'd never even have sent that email to the list.

Jake was never the end result. Jake was simply a necessary step to get me to Melinda.

There is no such thing as failure. There is no disaster. It really is stepping stones all the way.

29. How Does It Work?

I once believed things like 'stopping complaining' and 'feeling gratitude' and 'giving to others' and 'letting everything be okay' and the other instructions I gave in earlier books were prerequisites for becoming magic. Turns out, I was only half-right.

Sometimes, avoiding complaining, feeling gratitude and *trust* still work like a charm for me, dropping me instantly into that deep well of peace and wellbeing. Sometimes they don't do anything. There can be no prescription, no precise instruction for becoming magic that will work for all people at all times. Such a perfect instruction cannot exist. In itself, any technique has no more power for me than walking in the forest, listening to Irish fiddle music, smelling woodsmoke, or watching the final scene in *The Fellowship of the Ring*.

For some people, meditation or self-inquiry is a more reliable method for hooking up to magic. For some, it's playing music. But it absolutely isn't necessary to follow a technique at all. You can drop into that space completely without warning, while listening to a seminar speaker, reading a book, watching TV, even while washing the dishes.

I have come to see I don't need to actively stop complaining, because when I'm in touch with my inner magic, I just don't feel like complaining. I don't have to try hard to become less attached to the outcome of my creation attempts, because when I become magic, I'm simply not so attached to them. Not complaining, feeling gratitude, and letting everything be okay are what happen naturally and automatically when I get in touch with magic. And then, because I'm hooked up to the good stuff, I start not complaining and feeling gratitude naturally. So, the two reinforce each other. In themselves, those techniques and instructions have no power to do magic, but they can help get me in touch with the greatest power in the universe.

Doing magic, or manifesting, or magically creating is about getting in touch with that inner source of power and potential and resting in the perfection that is you. From here, everything starts looking sunny. You naturally start focussing on the good in your life and overlooking the rest. Everything looks *brighter*. Doing magic is about acting *from this perfect place*, going out in the world as a creator, as a magician, playing and experimenting, trying things and changing direction, seeing what wonderful things, people, and adventures you can find, all with a sense of 'I wonder what happens if I do this...'

But there's more.

Right from the beginning, when I created by 'becoming magic' and then taking inspired action in the direction of my goal, something amazing started happening, something that I couldn't explain by everyday means. It was as if *I wasn't alone.* When I opened myself up to this source of infinite potential, when I *became magic* and began creating my desire, the universe *helped me along.* It's as if for every move I made, every step I took, the universe took two, putting all the right people and places in my path. Everything started to feel enchanted, serendipitous, lucky.

These days, when I remain really deeply hooked up to my inner magic for long periods of time, it does often seem that things appear out of nowhere. Everything starts to go my way, and the universe genuinely seems sometimes to give me things. Ever since I got back from that session with Michael Neill, I have felt like King Midas because everything I touch turns to gold.

When my partner, Mike, started following the instructions in *Becoming Rich*, opportunities began to flood in from nowhere. Old university contacts, random Google searchers, and friends-of-friends-of-friends started calling him out of the blue wanting him to work for them. These people hadn't spoken to Mike for years (or *ever* in some cases), and he hadn't done anything to seek them out. Yet still, they went out of their way to find him, in their droves.

Experiences like this appear to go way beyond *'Things just seem better when you're in a good place'.* Even, *'When you do more stuff, more stuff happens'* doesn't really do it justice. The universe really does appear to step in to help with your endeavours. This is a phenomenon that has been noted again and again by writers and thinkers throughout history. As Joseph Campbell famously said, 'Follow your bliss and the universe will open doors where once there were only walls.'

As soon as I take inspired *action* (especially action outside my normal comfort zone) in the direction of my goal, the universe always conspires to help me out with resources, people, and fortuitous events. That is beyond doubt. And sometimes, that action can be something as simple as an attitude change or a decision. I'm not the first to notice this. Consider this wondrous quote from WH Murray:

'Concerning all acts of initiative (and creation), there is one elementary truth, the ignorance of which kills countless ideas and splendid plans: that the moment one definitely commits oneself, then **Providence moves too.** All sorts of things occur to help one that would never otherwise have occurred. A whole stream of events issues from the decision, raising in one's favour all manner of unforeseen incidents and meeting and material assistance which no man could have dreamt would come his way.' (Emphasis added.)

So now, putting my cards on the table: here is the game of magical creation explained according to my new understanding.

• By following instructions, trusting, meditating, or by other means, we *Become Magic.* We enter, hook up with, or tap into our inner magic, that great source of power, wisdom and wellbeing, that 'receiving state', that place throughout my life I have called *The Glimpse.*

- Because we are naturally less attached to the outcome of our efforts, we become bold and fearless, seeking out, noticing, and acting on the myriad opportunities presented to us. (This boldness is increased even further once we recognise the world doesn't have any power to hurt us.)

- We become likely to deem things good rather than bad and pick, out of the millions of possible things we could focus on, those things that we tend to regard as good.

- All this leads us to be infinitely more creative, proactive, powerful, and effective than we are when we think life will only improve when we get our desire.

- Plus, for good measure, 'the universe' steps in and gives us a hand along the way, offering just the right people, resources, and serendipitous circumstances.

- Thus, by a combination of massive, continued, and inspired *action*, and seeing only the good in life, and with a helping hand from the universe, we create loads of new stuff, new opportunities, and new adventures.

- Because our state of mind is so good, we tend to view this new stuff as good, and it appears that we are receiving everything we ever wanted.

- So we create what we want. But also, we *want what we create.*

This is my best explanation of what is going on when we successfully manifest stuff.

An exponentially increasing perfect storm of magic

30. Dancing with Life

But as of early 2017, there was still one great failed manifestation — one thing I had never managed to create using magic. A human life.

By the time Mike and I got together I was already over 40. By the time we got around to discussing starting a family, it was all a bit too late. Mike wasn't overly bothered either way. He's an agreeable chap at the worst of times, and his attitude was 'I'll be very happy to be a dad, and I'll be very happy to not be a dad'. But for me, it was different. I started to realise how much I wished I'd had another child. Robin was wonderful, a gift, but I'd always wanted a daughter to add to my family.

In my mid-40s, if not impossible, it was likely to be difficult. And as the months went by and no baby came, I did my best not to be disappointed and trust that everything was working out fine. But it was extremely difficult with this particular situation.

Was I up for multiple rounds of IVF, hormone injections, and possibly a child with health problems? I'm not sure I was. But more than that, there was a reason I realised I shouldn't even try. You see, after some years of letting nature takes its course, I was nearly 47. Even if by some miracle I did manage to get pregnant, I could be 48 by the time the baby was born.

This meant when the child was 15, I would be 63. When the child was only 30, I would be 78, which meant there was a good chance Mike and I would leave this child alone and parentless when it was still quite young. When Robin was little, one of my greatest fears was that I would die and leave him alone without a mother. How could I set myself on a path that made that nightmare scenario *likely*? I couldn't do it.

But still the ambivalence was there — I wanted a baby, but I knew it was a terrible idea, and it was becoming a worse idea every day. Even in my late 40s, there was still a mixture of disappointment and relief every month that I wasn't pregnant.

Of all the attempted manifestations, this was the one I seemed unable to remain unattached to. This was the dream I still yearned for. And perhaps that was what kept it away from me. Despite my magical abilities and all the incredible things I had been able to create, it seemed a human life was the one thing beyond my capabilities.

It seems there were some things you just can't manifest.

At the age of 48, I finally gave up. For so long, I had clung to the dream. I still fantasised about holding that little baby girl in my arms, looking at her big blue eyes, and realising my little family had grown. I'd even chosen a name, Darcie.

I loved this name so much I had considered using it as my pen name instead of Genevieve.

By now, most of my female friends were talking of menopausal symptoms and the pros and cons of HRT. Although I wasn't experiencing symptoms myself, I knew changes weren't far away. So I made the decision that my motherhood days were over. I gave up on my little baby girl, Darcie. There was no way around this one. A failed manifestation. This one hadn't come to be. The magic hadn't worked this time. I stopped feeling disappointed every month that I wasn't pregnant. I accepted middle age. I even made an appointment with a bioidentical hormone specialist to discuss my future options.

In June of last year, I took my mother to Ireland — a present for her 70th birthday. We spent a week in Galway, the Aran Islands, and Connemara. I absolutely love Ireland. The Irish must be my favourite people on the planet. Despite everything they have been through, as a nation they remain so upbeat and chipper, and the country has a genuine sense of magic about it. The whole place seems alive. If only my family would come with me, I'd move there in a heartbeat.

One afternoon my mother and I sat in the Cupán Tae tea shop at the bottom of town and had a real heart-to-heart. She asked me if Mike and I had ever thought about having children. I told her about my yearning for a little girl and my fears of dying and leaving the child alone. As I sat there, it dawned on me for the first time, that I truly was never going to have a baby girl. Feeling a little sad, I did what I always do when things don't seem to be going my way or when I'm unhappy. I fell deeply into trust. I trusted completely that my decision not to have a baby over the age of 45 had absolutely been the right thing to do. For possibly the first time since I got together with Mike, I accepted that I wasn't going to get my baby girl, not ever.

Mum and I left the tea shop and walked up Quay Street, heading back to our hotel. On the way, we stopped to listen to one of Galway's immensely talented street musicians. He was playing that variety of fiddle music that seems to speak straight to my heart, lift my soul, and connect me with heaven. In raptures, I stood listening to the beautiful music.

Then, my mobile phone rang. It was Robin.

'I've got something to tell you,' he said. 'Lizzie is pregnant. We've been for the scan. You're going to have a granddaughter.'

Okay, I *know* I can't claim to have manifested a baby into someone else's body. *I* didn't make the baby. Robin and Lizzie did that. But something very strange had happened here. Moments after finally accepting I would never again be a mother, I discovered my family was about to grow.

So what did happen? I have to hold up my hands and admit *I don't know*. Perhaps by accepting what I couldn't change, I got into the flow of the universe, rather than struggling against it. *Dancing with life,* as I have often called it. But for now, I'll fall back on my standard response — it's *magic.*

Despite being with my stuff-and-nonsense mother, a woman not prone to emotional outbursts, I stood there on the streets of Galway and wept tears of joy.

I was to get 'my' baby girl.

Okay, okay, so she wouldn't really be *mine*. But a little bit of me would be in that baby, she would be of my blood. A little girl was going to join my family. The things I had wanted to do with my daughter, I could do instead with this little girl. I could pay for her piano lessons, watch her school nativity plays, take her to museums, and teach her about magic. All without IVF, health problems, and sleepless nights. I didn't even need to get the morning sickness!

But that wasn't the end of it.

In the autumn of last year, Lizzie went into hospital. At 11 pm, the phone rang at home. 'Can you hear this?' Robin asked me. Then, on the other end of the phone, I heard the contented, snuggly drinking sounds of a new baby. Within an hour of her birth, I was holding my newborn granddaughter in my arms.

'What have you decided to call her?' I asked. And Robin told me she was to be called *Darcie.*

I was flabbergasted! I had not once told a living soul about my plans for baby names, not even Mike. And of all the names in the world, they had chosen the one name I had planned to call my own baby. Seriously, what are the chances? It's not even a common name. Other than ballerina Darcey Bussell, I have never heard of another.

The perfection in this is stunning. Being a grandmother at the age of 49 is *so* much better than being mother to a two-year-old at the age of 49. If only I had known!

Like Robin, Darcie is a happy, sunny child. She laughs a lot and sleeps well. She is impossibly pretty. She even has blue eyes like me, even though neither Robin nor Lizzie does. I will have to resist the temptation to spoil her dreadfully. My little family did grow in the most lovely way. As my mum likes to say, 'Darcie isn't actually *your* baby. But she is "a *bit* yours".' And so, now, I truly have received everything I ever asked for, *even a human life.*

I know there is a perfectly everyday explanation for what happened here. Robin and Lizzie had a baby, just like people do all over the world. People have babies. Women become grandmothers. It happens every day. So you might want to claim I never manifested anything. You might claim all I really ever did was get into a good place, become less fearful, and notice the beauty of this world.

But you know what? I'll take that, thanks. Because even if things only *seem* better when you're hooked up to magic — when you let go and trust in something greater — this is nothing to be disappointed about. This is nothing to be sad about. This is something to celebrate. This is fantastic. And it *is* so because of one indisputable fact:

Things *seeming* better is not inferior to things actually being better.

Things *seeming* better is *identical* to things actually being better.

31. It Really Is Magic

People use different terms to refer to what I call magic. It was only last year I discovered how perfect my choice of words turned out to be.

When I first started getting into magic, I was very lonely. As part of my push to find new friends I joined a local choir called Soulful Singing. It is not a performance choir, but rather a chance for a load of strangers to come together and sing for the sheer pleasure of it. I am not a good singer and have a very small vocal range. But I can hit the high notes, and hidden away amongst the other sopranos, my reedy voice would not sound out of place.

We sang folk songs, African songs, Celtic songs, and Buddhist chants, when I would completely lose myself in the music. My favourite piece was the Manjughosa mantra, a piece with harmonies so lovely, singing it would often put me in a good mood for the entire day. You can listen to the choir singing the chant for yourself here:

https://mahasukha.bandcamp.com/track/manjughosa-mantra-3

My first visit back to Soulful Singing after my awakening was to be quite a day. We sang the usual African songs, took our 15-minute break to drink coffee and chat, and then we were back in the room for an Irish song before the choir leader announced we would be doing the Manjughosa mantra to end the session. Inside, I smiled.

We began to sing. As the harmony rose up, I felt such an ecstasy at the beauty of the sound that tears came to my eyes, and my chest seemed to puff up with love. I was in The Glimpse, hooked up to that exquisitely perfect place inside me, filled with magic, basking in the perfection of the moment.

The words of the Manjughosa mantra are *Oṃ a ra pa ca na dhīḥ*. I don't have the first clue what they mean but that doesn't stop the mantra from working. Singing those words elicited a response in me of love and connection and joy. Any musicians out there will know what I am talking about.

And that's when the insight came to me.

All my attempts over the years — the meditation, the self-inquiry, the reading, the trying so hard to have a spiritual awakening — all that time, I had been trying to understand things with the wrong part of me. The part of me that didn't understand didn't need to understand. The part of me that didn't get it didn't need to get it. I had been acting like someone going along to the Soulful Singing choir and trying to grasp exactly what is meant by the words of the mantra, *Oṃ a ra pa ca na dhīḥ*, so they could encounter the same bliss that I do when I sing it. Without even realising, I'd been trying to understand rationally, intellectually, trapped in thought without knowing it.

Only then did I recognise the perfection of my decision to name this whole process *magic*. After all, how do you get someone like me, an 'overthinker', to see past their intellect? What's the best way to shut up the intellect of someone who has spent a lifetime over-intellectualising everything? *Give it something it can't possibly ever understand.* Give it something utterly ungraspable using rational thinking. Give it something so intangible and so unfathomable, it gives up trying to work things out.

I can think of no better concept for this purpose than *magic*.

All my life I've heard people, even spiritual people, reject the notion of 'magic'. The term is even bandied about as an insult. It comes with an association of nonsensicalness, irrationality, and fairy stories. Little wonder so many of us believed we were capable of doing magic as children but lost that ability. But when you reject magic and use it only as a derogatory term, you lose something of enormous value. In fact, I sometimes wonder why we don't make use of the concept more often.

And here's why.

Because an experience of inner magic is not something the intellectual mind can make sense of, the only way to glimpse it is to *ignore* the logical arguments of the intellectual mind and allow the thinking to settle just long enough to let the light shine through. And this, it turned out, was what I was inadvertently doing when I chose to believe in magic. I ignored the protestations of my rational mind and trusted in something unseen, something inexplicable.

The concept of magic had allowed me to let go of those preconceptions and judgements, settling my overactive mind, my doubts and worries, silencing that ever-questioning internal chatter. Simply by *calling* it by a name that was ungraspable, intangible, and hopelessly vague — *magic* — I was able to *let go* of *having to understand it*. I was able to stop trying to work it out. To calm that constantly active mind with its questions, questions, questions. To allow my intellect to rest, to stop it from getting in there, taking charge, interfering and messing everything up. In doing so, I opened myself to any and all possibilities, whether or not they fit with science, logic, philosophy, my current understanding, or anything else.

Magic defies precise description, ignores logic, bypasses science. My new insights would never be scientifically verifiable, not because they were nonsense, but because the defining characteristic of scientific methodology is its objectivity, and objectivity has no place when investigating a phenomenon that can only be accessed through subjective experience.

It didn't matter whether I believed in magic as a separate entity, force, power or place. It was still immensely valuable as *a concept*. Because, as a concept alone, it allowed me to *shut down the thinking*, if only momentarily. And that's when it happened. That's when the thoughts settled, the clouds parted, the truth bubbled up and revealed itself to me.

It's the power in *I don't know.*
It's the power in *I haven't a clue.*
It's the power of *God moves in mysterious ways.*
It's the power of a blank mind, no preconceptions, and infinite possibilities.
It's the power of trusting without question.

And by trusting in magic without question, I was able to change my whole life.

Call it something else if you like. Choose your term. Pick your description. Call it *trust*. Call it *letting go*. Call it *clearing your mind*. Call it *being open to all possibilities*. Call it *blue-sky thinking*. People trying to explain this stuff tend to fall back on metaphor because it's really the only way of communicating such intangible ideas. Well, 'magic' turned out to be my perfect metaphor. I didn't need to be woo-woo and away with the fairies to see the value in a concept like this.

Magic was the perfect term, even for those who don't believe in magic.

In fact, magic is the perfect term, *especially* for those who don't believe in magic! After all, the stronger a person's aversion to the concept of magic, the louder their intellectual mind is shouting. That voice needs to be quieted.

Now I know why I ended up rejecting the overly rational intellectualising of philosophy. This method of inquiry was great for some purposes, but it was also stifling, overwhelming, and ended up dominating my mind so completely for so many years that the quieter, gentler, *truer* voice couldn't be heard. When I learned to drop my attachment to logical argument and to *feel* what is really there… I was able to drop into a whole different world of knowing, a whole different *way* of knowing.

There was no longer any need to hide away in the shadows behind a pen name. There was no need to be slightly embarrassed by my belief in such a cosmic idea. And on that day at Soulful Singing, after the Manjughosa mantra, I came to realise something else: it was *essential* that magic remain mysterious to me. I didn't *want* to find a more rational explanation. It was this very lack of explicability, this otherworldliness that had made magic such a powerful notion.

So, I'm never going to get into any arguments with anyone over the existence of magic or whether there is a better term to describe it. Don't ask me to explain how magic *really* works or what it *really* is. I can't and won't tell you. If you have a completely scientific explanation for everything I have described, that's really, really fine with me.

I've always been completely open to the idea of there being another way of describing what I call 'magic', and if you want to attempt it with science, more power to you. I don't think you'll succeed, because science is simply unfit for this purpose. And, to be honest, any scientific attempt to describe the weirdness that is human experience is going to end up so contrived, *it might as well be magic anyway.*

And, given a choice between a life filled with magic or a life filled with science, *I choose magic.*

32. What Is Life Like Now?

So how does life look for me today?

As I sit here, in my favourite café, and reflect on the last few years, I can hardly believe all this has happened to me. While recounting this story, it has sometimes felt like I'm talking about someone else's life. The bleak depressions that once plagued me seem like they happened to some other person. The changes I have made, the places magic has taken me — it's astounding to consider how far I've come. But most mind-blowing of all is how far I've come since *this time last year*. It's just shy of a year since that desolate moment outside the pub where I thought it might be my last day on earth. It has been a whole year without a depression, almost a whole year without even a bad mood!

These days, I still have the odd low moment. But it lasts minutes or hours, rather than weeks or months. Sometimes, I drop out of this understanding. I lose my connection to magic. I fall back into the normal world, forget where my experience is really coming from, and start believing the world has the power to bring me down. But whereas life was once one long struggle, with brief periods of joy and connection, now those poles are reversed. If I fall back into worrying and criticising, I spot my mistake pretty early on. I notice I've fallen for the illusion again, I return immediately to a better understanding of how life works, and peace reigns once again. If I hadn't had this understanding, every bad mood could trigger a downward spiral into depression. Now that I understand where my experience is really coming from, monthlong depressions don't make sense anymore.

The gratitude I experience now on a daily basis is profound.

At this point in time, I genuinely do have every 'thing' I've ever asked for. And I'm not talking only about the ordinary material things like money and houses and cars. I'm talking about things like a growing sense of fearlessness, a bigger family, spiritual awakening, a sense of community. Even my weirdest and most incomprehensible wish to 'live in The Glimpse' has pretty much come true.

It is these less tangible but infinitely more valuable things that have enriched my life in a way I didn't know was possible. Aston Martins, first-class tickets, and bottles of champagne are nice. They are *really* nice. But they are *nothing* compared to the knowledge I'll never suffer depression again. Sometimes I find myself smiling at the thought of the life I have to look forward to — a life without fear of things going wrong. Could there be any manifestation more fabulous?

And the perfection of it is this...

All the hardship — the bad times when I thought things were going wrong, the depressions that floored me, the snap-backs that nearly broke me — have *all been worth it*. But not only were they worth it, they were *necessary*. The truth is, I could never have got here *without* those depressions, disappointments, snap-backs, and despairing moods. It was precisely these unwanted events that set me on the path I took. All were essential stepping stones on a journey that has led to this exquisite moment here, sitting here in my favourite café, with every material possession I could ever want and a stunning spiritual awakening to boot, looking forward to the rest of my life with so much enthusiasm I can hardly stand to go to bed at night. Life is so much fun these days, I don't want to waste time sleeping.

One thing I can say for sure, life would have turned out very differently had I not believed in magic.

I'm not going to be as crass as to reel off a list of the material goods I have manifested since my awakening. I'm not going to tell you about the gold-plated houses I've bought, a different Aston Martin for every day of the week, and all the diamond-encrusted teapots. These days, I'm not creating bigger and better and flashier. In fact, I have become remarkably uninterested in creating any more fancy stuff.

I never wanted a house so big it has rooms I never go into. I wanted a house with character, stripped wood floors, high ceilings, and an open fire, somewhere good for the cats, close to my mum and Robin, in a safe and friendly community. And that's exactly what I have.

I never wanted a Ferrari or a £200k Tesla. I always wanted an Aston Martin DB7 Vantage — in my opinion, the most beautiful car ever created. And that's exactly what I have. A car so pretty, when the sun shines across its organic curves it sometimes takes my breath away.

I have over a dozen completely separate revenue streams, giving me a passive income that allows me to work when I want, and *if* I want.

So my attitude to more possessions is kind of 'been there, done that'. And to be honest, now that I know material things have no actual power to make me feel good, I can't be bothered to create them anymore.

But I'm not done yet.

Oh no, not by a long shot. I'm still going to create. I'm still going to be doing magic. I'm still going to be making things happen and bringing new things into my life. But these days, I'm looking for a tad more of a challenge. You see, I'm now setting about creating things, doing things, and bringing about situations that once upon a time would have been unthinkable for me.

The first of these is 'going public', something I flatly refused to do for years for fear it would 'break the magic', or that everything would go wrong, and I'd end up humiliated. I now know this is impossible — the world can't make me feel anything, so things can't *ever* go wrong. This means there is no need for anonymity anymore. I'll be creating an online course, recording podcasts, writing blog posts, and sharing Instagram photos. The hiding is over.

But the most unbelievable plan is this — I intend to start performing speaking engagements. I realise this may sound like a fairly small thing for some of you. But not for me. You see, I am one of those who has spent a lifetime truly fearing death less than getting up and speaking in public. So this creation seems like the craziest, most ambitious, and impossible plan I have ever had.

And here's the great thing — I've no idea how I'm going to achieve it! I don't know how a person goes from an extreme phobia to competency in public speaking. But that's not going to stop me. I know that all I need to do is hook up to the magic, take steps in the direction of my goal, and have a 'let everything be okay' attitude to life. The rest is down to the universe. I know it will respond. And because this is all for fun, it really doesn't matter one way or the other whether I get my goal. And the delicious irony is this lack of attachment will make me all the more likely to succeed.

So now that I've become cosmic and awakened and uninterested in material stuff, does this mean I'm going to get all pious, lock myself away, renounce all my worldly goods and sit on a mountain, or hide in a cave for 30 years in a blissed-out state of spiritual loveliness?

I was always slightly afraid of this. For a long time, I did think if I ever had a spiritual awakening, I'd lose my interest in pure, unadulterated fun. I worried I'd no longer be interested in playing samba, dancing to Irish fiddle music, driving Astons, laughing at puerile jokes, and drinking wine on the beach. I also heard that spiritual people become uninterested in material possessions, luxury, and creature comforts.

I remember being at a Zen retreat, and a group of us were arranging the *zafus* (the cushions used to sit on for meditation) in preparation for the evening's session. We were laughing and joking around, racing each other to see how fast we could lay the cushions. One of the senseis (teachers) heard our laughs, entered the room, and proceeded to chastise us for our lack of respect and our childishness. *Didn't we know we were disrespecting the very seat of the Buddha?* It was incidents like this that led me to think if I became too spiritual, I'd become boring, sanctimonious, and serious.

Spirituality or stuff? Spirituality or silliness? Spirituality or fun? Which was more important?

Only quite recently it has dawned on me: *I don't have to choose!*

The magic *I* am concerned with is not serious or sanctimonious. It is not stuck-up or aloof. As far as I can tell, there is no greater way to stay in the 'receiving state' than to laugh. And you know, I *really* can't imagine the Buddha being offended by people playing with cushions.

I've come to realise it's extremely important that I don't take life or myself too seriously. I talk nonsense a lot of the time. I laugh out loud — a lot. When something moves me, I help or I give money. If it doesn't, I don't. But generally speaking, I take life very light-heartedly indeed. I continue to be very silly. People have sometimes berated me for this. But there is no way I am going to give up my silliness in deference to their seriousness. The world doesn't need another serious person.

I'm not giving up my stuff either. Hiding away in a cave or getting rid of material possessions is not a prerequisite to or a consequence of becoming spiritual. It is a *choice.* 'You cannot be spiritual and rich' is *not* a fundamental truth, as some people like to proclaim. It is the articulation of a *thought,* nothing more. I suspect those who told me spirituality must be separate from getting rich had simply been inflicting their own morality or feelings of guilt on me. And to be honest, that's not very spiritual at all.

Plus, the fact is, it is *only* by becoming wealthy that I have had the money, time, and freedom to do a lot of good (in the conventional sense). Not only am I able to support numerous charities and worthy causes, I am also able to make ethical buying choices. Free-Range, Cruelty-Free, Fair Trade, Locally-Produced, or Organic goods don't come into the picture when you don't have enough to eat. So, while you won't find me bemoaning the state of the world or sharing my political opinions, that doesn't mean I'm not doing my best to live a good and ethical life.

But you know, the best thing about creating things is that *it's fun.* It's *interesting.* It's an *adventure.* Magic is the game I choose to play. It's my 'thing'. It's not *everyone's* thing. Some people play the science game. Some play the psychology game. Some play the reiki or the astrology or the chakra game. Some play the working-hard-all-your-life game. All work well in certain situations and less so in others. But I'm going to keep on playing the magic game. Since I've got to play one game or another, it might as well be a fun one.

A time might come when I start to see that possessions, partners, jobs, friends, houses, and money are so unimportant I won't even care whether they are there or not. Maybe then, I'll go and hide in a cave.

But until I get there, I'm going to keep on playing!

33. The Perfection of You

If you believe deep down that you are special, this is not some delusion; it reflects an underlying truth about you and the immensity of your true underlying power. It doesn't matter how old you are or what colour you are; it doesn't matter how educated or intelligent you are; it doesn't matter if you are considered beautiful or ugly; it doesn't matter whether you were born into extreme poverty and are living in a wooden shack or mud hut. I put it to you that you are still perfect, divine, and unbelievably powerful. Somewhere, deep down, your greatness is sitting...and waiting (Becoming Magic, Chapter One)

When I read back through my work, through books and articles I have written, it sometimes seems like I'm reading someone else's words. I know I wrote those words because I recorded them first in my journal. But the truth is, I don't remember doing it. When those words came to me, all I knew was they came with a feeling of complete 'rightness'. But I was always the first to admit the four books I wrote in the Course in Manifesting series were somewhat naïvely written; they were just my best approximations of what I took to be true. At the time, I had no real idea of the significance of what I was writing.

But now, I do.

As I sit here in my favourite coffee shop, finishing up this book, it occurs to me that I should stop talking about myself and turn the focus more in your direction. You've heard me talk about myself for 50,000 words, but *what's in it for you?*

The truth is, my own story was incidental to my real motivation for writing *Becoming Genevieve*. The whole book has been an attempt to point you in the direction of an impossibly fantastic 'place' within you. As a child I called it *The Glimpse*. Others call it innate wellbeing, or the source, or divine mind, or the true self, or even *God*.

I call it *magic*.

What I'm about to say is 100% true whether you believe it or not. I can say this with absolute certainty, not because it sounds nice, or because I've heard someone else talk about it, or because it's what I'm 'supposed' to say, but because it comes from *my direct personal experience*. These are not random words that came to me one morning either — this is what I'm seeing right now, right at this minute.

Okay, here goes...

Inside of me, you, and every other human being, is a place of utter perfection, a well of love and joy and wisdom, an oasis of wellbeing where existence itself feels exquisite. It's also a place of complete and perfect *wisdom*. I always used to think 'wisdom' a rather pompous-sounding term, but now I can see no better term to describe what I'm trying to point to. Because you can ask for an answer to any question you have ever wished to ask and get the most perfect answer. This place also contains anything you have ever wanted to feel, and everything you have ever wanted to experience can be found in this place. I say 'place' because I don't really have an ideal word for what I am trying to point you to. In many ways, it is more like a state of being, a state you can slip into. And in other ways, it isn't like any of these things, because it *is* you.

What I am speaking of is like an elementary characteristic of who you are, your core. The essence of you. It is what lies beneath. The pure you-ness, without all the fears, anxieties, likes and dislikes, broken dreams, and unfulfilled desires. Before the beliefs and disbeliefs, the hopes and theories, the attitudes and worries, and everything you think about yourself. It is before any of the external world appears to rush in.

It is the real you. The quintessential you.

I'm talking about what Sydney Banks called Divine Mind. I'm talking about Big Mind. I'm talking about a direct experience of the universe, of the source of creation itself. I'm talking about plunging into what I have previously (and somewhat erroneously) called 'the receiving state' and living from that place.

I'm talking about a direct communion with magic. *Real* magic.

If you like to talk in these terms, you might even say it is a direct experience with God.

So why can't you see or sense it all the time?

The reason is always the same — you are far more tangled up in your thinking than you know. Your thoughts appear so real, so concrete, so immediate that they are all you can see. You are lost in them. But below and behind the intellect, under the thoughts, in the background sits this beautiful magical state. It's right there now. It's *always* there. It's just that some of your thoughts are shouting too loudly for you to hear it.

You, me, all of us have started believing our thoughts are our world, taking them as truth, allowing them to run and rule and ruin our lives. Your mind is almost certainly trying to jump in right now, like a bossy child — 'Let me look at this,' it says. 'Stand aside. I'll work it out. I'm all that matters here. It's all about me, me, me.'

There's only ever one way to get a look at the truth — allow those thoughts to settle. You won't know how distracting your thoughts really are until they clear, and you can experience life without their interference. Then you'll see for yourself that this magical state was *always* there, just waiting to bubble back up to the surface. It's built-in, part of the design of you as a human being.

It is this settling, this tuning in, this noticing, this seeing past the words and thoughts and worries and cares and judgements that allows magic to show itself... *This* is the process I call *Becoming Magic*. When you can 'tune in' to this humming, background magical energy, life seems somehow more beautiful. Everything makes sense. You can see things, know things, understand things your rational mind can't grasp. You don't have to do anything or learn anything because you already *have* what you are looking for, and you already *are* all that you are looking for.

And, you know, there's a really fabulous consequence of what I've just said.

You may be living on benefits or welfare and surviving on handouts from the food bank. You may have had a childhood of depravation or terrible abuse. You might be in prison. You might be plagued with mental illness, depression, or terrible anxiety. You might have witnessed horrific violence and endured experiences that still haunt your dreams.

But you are not... *broken*. Not ever.

I'm not saying this to cheer you up with insincere platitudes or fake compassion. This is not about forced sympathy or self-congratulatory, puffed-up Facebook kindness. I am saying this because it's true. You are perfect.

Yes, I'm talking to *you*.

It's true because I've seen it. This is as real as it gets.

On the outside, there are vast differences between us all, materially and otherwise. But underneath, at our core, when it comes to what really matters, we are all the same, and we are perfect. *All of us.*

None of your skills, intelligence, advantages, or privileges, and none of your character flaws, disabilities, disadvantages, and seemingly insurmountable problems will make *any difference* to your ability to access, see, and experience the exquisite truth of your own perfection, *and the perfection of every single one of us.*

When you see this, really see it, you will understand how a person can have compassion for each and every human being alive. You will know how it is possible to love someone you have never met. You will see the criminal, the bully, and those who have wronged you with new eyes. You will experience a oneness with the whole of humanity that goes beyond and before any of the horrible crimes or the good deeds anyone has committed. It's the kindest truth: we really are all 100% equal.

Once you have found this place, you will have what you need to go about creating an exceptional life for yourself. And you will then see your life anew, with excitement, like a child again.

You will return to the place I described at the very beginning of my first book, *Becoming Magic,* which described an existence characterised by magic, wonder, and joy. This time, you will know that my description of that place within you that is perfect, magic, and powerful goes far beyond motivational peptalk. You won't only hope or suspect or believe, you will *know,* deep in your heart, as true as you know night follows day, that this place is *real.*

You'll also be able to create things with an ease you probably can't even comprehend right now. Once you get the inspiration to create your desire, and *start acting on it,* you're going to discover just how much the universe is willing to help you out. It will offer you opportunities and resources, serendipitous circumstances, putting all the right people and events in your way to make everything easier. It will give you insights that will blow your mind. It will provide you with suggestions you might never ever have dreamed of. It will provide you with fantastic confidence, inspire you to act, and to go off in directions you never would have dreamed. Rather than passively calling on the universe to give you what you want, you'll be motivated to create those things yourself and excited about the steps you're going to take to get them.

You may not have had a vast insight into the nature of the human experience while reading this book. But if there is the merest ping of recognition, a chime of resonance, a faint light going on somewhere, that is enough. That's all I wanted to achieve. My job is done. *Because that's how it starts.*

Sometimes, people are lucky enough to have an immediate, unsought awakening experience. Often, like Eckhart Tolle or Byron Katie, this happens during a period of extreme stress or depression. For others, it is entirely spontaneous and without reason or warning, as it was with my friend Ella.

Another way to see these truths is via a sudden and life-changing insight that comes about on hearing a message spoken by some guru or teacher. Insights like this come when the words resonate with a deeper wisdom within you. Something in you wakes up, and a truth you already knew but had forgotten is able to burst through. This is the way it was with Syd Banks, the founder of The Three Principles movement. It was how it was with Michael Neill, the man who was a great catalyst in my own awakening.

It's *not* how it was with me.

The truth came much more slowly into my life. It came in fragments, starting with the *Glimpses*, through working with the receiving state, the experience of meeting Michael Neill, and the various large and small epiphanies that occurred over the years. It gradually patched itself together until it formed an untidy whole. Now, I have a much fuller picture, and lots of the gaps have been filled in, pieced together like a jigsaw. These days, when I have new insights, I am able to slot them smoothly into the whole picture. It's a picture that's becoming clearer and clearer all the time. But I am light years away from a complete picture. The learning will continue until the day I die (and maybe beyond).

Some of you, similarly, won't have that initial life-changing, thunderbolt moment. For some of you, the magic will creep up almost imperceptibly, and you'll simply find yourself with a sense of clarity and rightness. Don't imagine you have to have a sudden world-changing experience for it to count. In fact, I think overexpectation can work to keep the truth from showing itself. For much of my life, I was searching so hard for that earth-shattering, life-defining moment that I didn't notice the bits and pieces of truth that were doing their best to shout out at me.

So the truth is, at this point, it really doesn't matter if you don't understand or accept a single word of what I'm talking about. Wherever you are in your understanding or ability, where you are right now, reading this book, at this precise moment in time *is perfect*. Everything in your life that has happened has led to this moment. It has all been necessary, and it has all been worth it. You are in exactly the right place. Just take that in for a moment — everything is working out perfectly.

Consider this passage from one of my early books,

I decided to stop the dibble dabbling. Something was happening, and I was never going to understand what until I stopped messing around and took things seriously. I let go of all the dogma and stopped reading new books. I had read enough. It was time to look at this whole thing in a more considered way. I was not going to understand it by reading. I was going to understand it by seeing how it plays out in the real world, in my world. I began to loosen up on the strict adherence to someone else's 'rules'. I soon saw that there were no real laws here, no strict rules.

Instead, I asked myself 'what is true for you?'

It's incredible to look back and think about this little question, knowing what I do now. As the years have gone on, I have continued to ask this question. And as I have done so, my understanding has grown and matured and gone off in the most incredible directions.

So, let me ask you: Is there just a small part of you that suspects I am telling the truth?

Is something ringing true?

If something —*anything* — resonates, there's a reason for that. The deeper, wiser part of you understands perfectly what I'm saying even when your conscious mind is shouting objections. *This* is the reason the words resonate with you. The truth is, on some level, *you already know this stuff.* There's a part of you that could think these thoughts, say these words. In fact, *you could have written this book yourself.*

You could, couldn't you?

The part that jumps in and says that's nonsense — just ignore that voice. It's your intellect taking charge again. When the voice starts to quieten, and you feel yourself settling down, stay there. Just *trust.* Let it all wash over you. Let it be. Whenever you notice a little smile appearing on your lips and you don't know why — just sit with it... and wait.

When the student is ready, the teacher will appear.

Except that your teacher isn't me. Your own guru, and the source of all the wisdom you will ever need, is *you.*

I mean this literally and completely.

To those that sense a whisper of truth in what I've just said, know that if you keep looking in this direction, pretty soon you won't have to take my word for it anymore. You'll see the truth in your own experience with a clarity that goes way beyond the judgements of your intellectual mind.

You'll have a *Glimpse of Magic.*

If you don't see it yet, that's fine. You won't 'get it'…until you do. And as long as you *trust me,* we're going to get along fine. Understanding will come…in time. Stick with me. I'll do right by you.

So please stay with me on this new and unfamiliar path. Come along for the ride, because you might find paradise at its end. You may get everything you ever wanted. And you know what? That's just the beginning.

That's when the fun *really* starts.

Where to Go from Here…

You might be wondering, *But what do I do next?*

I am busy creating all sorts of resources to help you on your journey. In the coming months I'll be creating podcasts, blog posts, and all manner of goodies. So get on my mailing list, visit the website, keep in touch. If you need something a little more structured, register your interest for my first ever *Becoming Magic Online Program.*

If you've had enough of listening to me, I can point you in the direction of some excellent teachers. If you want to learn about Sydney Banks and The Three Principles, Jack Pransky's *Somebody Should Have Told Us!* is an excellent place to start. I can also recommend *The Inside-Out Revolution* by Michael Neill, *One Thought Changes Everything* by Mara Gleason, or anything by the man himself, Sydney Banks. If you're anywhere near the Lake District, get in touch with Jenny Anderson and Dave Elleray, who run some fantastic retreats in stunning countryside. But it's really up to you how to do it.

I know full well that I have lost some of you in writing this book. You may think I'm talking utter and complete nonsense. Some of you will already be working out what to write in an email you are planning to send, telling me exactly how and why you disagree with me, and where you think I have gone wrong. But please don't write that email. You will be wasting your time because I am not offering any theories or opinions to which you can object. The goal of this book was not to convince you of anything or argue for a particular interpretation or point of view. Simply put, there is nothing to disagree *with*. I'm trying to point you to something, to show you something, but I'm not trying to *convince* you of anything.

All that's ever needed is for your thoughts to settle long enough for the magic to shine through. You may wish to walk in nature, go for a long drive to nowhere, sit in coffee shops, or sing in a choir. You may want to check out Mooji or Eckhart Tolle, do self-inquiry, or you may like to meditate. Or… you may like to stick with me and see if we can't sort this thing out between us.

If you hate every word of what I'm saying, that's fine too. Put the book down and move on. I'm sorry to lose you as a reader, but hopefully one day you'll come back to me.

Okay, still with me? Good.

Keep listening. Keep reading.

The magic is right here, right now.

www.becomingmagic.com

Made in the USA
Lexington, KY
30 December 2018